ISBN 0-8373-1848-3

C-1848   CAREER EXAMINATION SERIES

This is your
PASSBOOK® for...

Administrative Assistant I

Test Preparation Study Guide

Questions & Answers

NLC

NATIONAL LEARNING CORPORATION

(516) 921-8888
(800) 645-6337
FAX: (516) 921-8743
www.passbooks.com
sales @ passbooks.com
info @ passbooks.com

PRINTED IN THE UNITED STATES OF AMERICA

PASSBOOK®

NOTICE

PASSBOOK SERIES®

THE *PASSBOOK SERIES®* has been created to prepare applicants and candidates for the ultimate academic battlefield – the examination room.

At some time in our lives, each and every one of us may be required to take an examination – for validation, matriculation, admission, qualification, registration, certification, or licensure.

Based on the assumption that every applicant or candidate has met the basic formal educational standards, has taken the required number of courses, and read the necessary texts, the *PASSBOOK SERIES®* furnishes the one special preparation which may assure passing with confidence, instead of failing with insecurity. Examination questions – together with answers – are furnished as the basic vehicle for study so that the mysteries of the examination and its compounding difficulties may be eliminated or diminished by a sure method.

This book is meant to help you pass your examination provided that you qualify and are serious in your objective.

The entire field is reviewed through the huge store of content information which is succinctly presented through a provocative and challenging approach – the question-and-answer method.

A climate of success is established by furnishing the correct answers at the end of each test.

You soon learn to recognize types of questions, forms of questions, and patterns of questioning. You may even begin to anticipate expected outcomes.

You perceive that many questions are repeated or adapted so that you can gain acute insights, which may enable you to score many sure points.

You learn how to confront new questions, or types of questions, and to attack them confidently and work out the correct answers.

You note objectives and emphases, and recognize pitfalls and dangers, so that you may make positive educational adjustments.

Moreover, you are kept fully informed in relation to new concepts, methods, practices, and directions in the field.

You discover that you are actually taking the examination all the time: you are preparing for the examination by "taking" an examination, not by reading extraneous and/or supererogatory textbooks.

In short, this PASSBOOK®, used directedly, should be an important factor in helping you to pass your test.

ADMINISTRATIVE ASSISTANT I

DUTIES
   Performs administrative staff work involving varied
assignments for an administrative supervisor necessary
for the operation of a department; performs related work
as required.

SCOPE OF THE WRITTEN TEST
   The written test will be designed to test for knowledge,
skills, and/or abilities in such areas as:
   1. Office management;
   2. Supervision;
   3. Preparing written material; and
   4. Grammar, usage, punctuation and spelling.

———

HOW TO TAKE A TEST

I. YOU MUST PASS AN EXAMINATION

A. WHAT EVERY CANDIDATE SHOULD KNOW

Examination applicants often ask us for help in preparing for the written test. What can I study in advance? What kinds of questions will be asked? How will the test be given? How will the papers be graded?

As an applicant for a civil service examination, you may be wondering about some of these things. Our purpose here is to suggest effective methods of advance study and to describe civil service examinations.

Your chances for success on this examination can be increased if you know how to prepare. Those "pre-examination jitters" can be reduced if you know what to expect. You can even experience an adventure in good citizenship if you know why civil service exams are given.

B. WHY ARE CIVIL SERVICE EXAMINATIONS GIVEN?

Civil service examinations are important to you in two ways. As a citizen, you want public jobs filled by employees who know how to do their work. As a job seeker, you want a fair chance to compete for that job on an equal footing with other candidates. The best-known means of accomplishing this two-fold goal is the competitive examination.

Exams are widely publicized throughout the nation. They may be administered for jobs in federal, state, city, municipal, town or village governments or agencies.

Any citizen may apply, with some limitations, such as the age or residence of applicants. Your experience and education may be reviewed to see whether you meet the requirements for the particular examination. When these requirements exist, they are reasonable and applied consistently to all applicants. Thus, a competitive examination may cause you some uneasiness now, but it is your privilege and safeguard.

C. HOW ARE CIVIL SERVICE EXAMS DEVELOPED?

Examinations are carefully written by trained technicians who are specialists in the field known as "psychological measurement," in consultation with recognized authorities in the field of work that the test will cover. These experts recommend the subject matter areas or skills to be tested; only those knowledges or skills important to your success on the job are included. The most reliable books and source materials available are used as references. Together, the experts and technicians judge the difficulty level of the questions.

Test technicians know how to phrase questions so that the problem is clearly stated. Their ethics do not permit "trick" or "catch" questions. Questions may have been tried out on sample groups, or subjected to statistical analysis, to determine their usefulness.

Written tests are often used in combination with performance tests, ratings of training and experience, and oral interviews. All of these measures combine to form the best-known means of finding the right person for the right job.

II. HOW TO PASS THE WRITTEN TEST

A. NATURE OF THE EXAMINATION

To prepare intelligently for civil service examinations, you should know how they differ from school examinations you have taken. In school you were assigned certain definite pages to read or subjects to cover. The examination questions were quite detailed and usually emphasized memory. Civil service exams, on the other hand, try to discover your present ability to perform the duties of a position, plus your potentiality to learn these duties. In other words, a civil service exam attempts to predict how successful you will be. Questions cover such a broad area that they cannot be as minute and detailed as school exam questions.

In the public service similar kinds of work, or positions, are grouped together in one "class." This process is known as *position-classification*. All the positions in a class are paid according to the salary range for that class. One class title covers all of these positions, and they are all tested by the same examination.

B. FOUR BASIC STEPS

1) Study the announcement

How, then, can you know what subjects to study? Our best answer is: "Learn as much as possible about the class of positions for which you've applied." The exam will test the knowledge, skills and abilities needed to do the work.

Your most valuable source of information about the position you want is the official exam announcement. This announcement lists the training and experience qualifications. Check these standards and apply only if you come reasonably close to meeting them.

The brief description of the position in the examination announcement offers some clues to the subjects which will be tested. Think about the job itself. Review the duties in your mind. Can you perform them, or are there some in which you are rusty? Fill in the blank spots in your preparation.

Many jurisdictions preview the written test in the exam announcement by including a section called "Knowledge and Abilities Required," "Scope of the Examination," or some similar heading. Here you will find out specifically what fields will be tested.

2) Review your own background

Once you learn in general what the position is all about, and what you need to know to do the work, ask yourself which subjects you already know fairly well and which need improvement. You may wonder whether to concentrate on improving your strong areas or on building some background in your fields of weakness. When the announcement has specified "some knowledge" or "considerable knowledge," or has used adjectives like "beginning principles of…" or "advanced … methods," you can get a clue as to the number and difficulty of questions to be asked in any given field. More questions, and hence broader coverage, would be included for those subjects which are more important in the work. Now weigh your strengths and weaknesses against the job requirements and prepare accordingly.

3) Determine the level of the position

Another way to tell how intensively you should prepare is to understand the level of the job for which you are applying. Is it the entering level? In other words, is this the position in which beginners in a field of work are hired? Or is it an intermediate or advanced level? Sometimes this is indicated by such words as "Junior" or "Senior" in the class title. Other jurisdictions use Roman numerals to designate the level – Clerk I, Clerk II, for example. The word "Supervisor" sometimes appears in the title. If the level is not indicated by the title, check the description of duties. Will you be working under very close supervision, or will you have responsibility for independent decisions in this work?

4) Choose appropriate study materials

Now that you know the subjects to be examined and the relative amount of each subject to be covered, you can choose suitable study materials. For beginning level jobs, or even advanced ones, if you have a pronounced weakness in some aspect of your training, read a modern, standard textbook in that field. Be sure it is up to date and has general coverage. Such books are normally available at your library, and the librarian will be glad to help you locate one. For entry-level positions, questions of appropriate difficulty are chosen – neither highly advanced questions, nor those too simple. Such questions require careful thought but not advanced training.

If the position for which you are applying is technical or advanced, you will read more advanced, specialized material. If you are already familiar with the basic principles of your field, elementary textbooks would waste your time. Concentrate on advanced textbooks and technical periodicals. Think through the concepts and review difficult problems in your field.

These are all general sources. You can get more ideas on your own initiative, following these leads. For example, training manuals and publications of the government agency which employs workers in your field can be useful, particularly for technical and professional positions. A letter or visit to the government department involved may result in more specific study suggestions, and certainly will provide you with a more definite idea of the exact nature of the position you are seeking.

III. KINDS OF TESTS

Tests are used for purposes other than measuring knowledge and ability to perform specified duties. For some positions, it is equally important to test ability to make adjustments to new situations or to profit from training. In others, basic mental abilities not dependent on information are essential. Questions which test these things may not appear as pertinent to the duties of the position as those which test for knowledge and information. Yet they are often highly important parts of a fair examination. For very general questions, it is almost impossible to help you direct your study efforts. What we can do is to point out some of the more common of these general abilities needed in public service positions and describe some typical questions.

1) General information

Broad, general information has been found useful for predicting job success in some kinds of work. This is tested in a variety of ways, from vocabulary lists to questions about current events. Basic background in some field of work, such as sociology or economics, may be sampled in a group of questions. Often these are principles which have become familiar to most persons through exposure rather than through formal training. It is difficult to advise you how to study for these questions; being alert to the world around you is our best suggestion.

2) Verbal ability

An example of an ability needed in many positions is verbal or language ability. Verbal ability is, in brief, the ability to use and understand words. Vocabulary and grammar tests are typical measures of this ability. Reading comprehension or paragraph interpretation questions are common in many kinds of civil service tests. You are given a paragraph of written material and asked to find its central meaning.

3) Numerical ability

Number skills can be tested by the familiar arithmetic problem, by checking paired lists of numbers to see which are alike and which are different, or by interpreting charts and graphs. In the latter test, a graph may be printed in the test booklet which you are asked to use as the basis for answering questions.

4) Observation

A popular test for law-enforcement positions is the observation test. A picture is shown to you for several minutes, then taken away. Questions about the picture test your ability to observe both details and larger elements.

5) Following directions

In many positions in the public service, the employee must be able to carry out written instructions dependably and accurately. You may be given a chart with several columns, each column listing a variety of information. The questions require you to carry out directions involving the information given in the chart.

6) Skills and aptitudes

Performance tests effectively measure some manual skills and aptitudes. When the skill is one in which you are trained, such as typing or shorthand, you can practice. These tests are often very much like those given in business school or high school courses. For many of the other skills and aptitudes, however, no short-time preparation can be made. Skills and abilities natural to you or that you have developed throughout your lifetime are being tested.

Many of the general questions just described provide all the data needed to answer the questions and ask you to use your reasoning ability to find the answers. Your best preparation for these tests, as well as for tests of facts and ideas, is to be at your physical and mental best. You, no doubt, have your own methods of getting into an exam-taking mood and keeping "in shape." The next section lists some ideas on this subject.

IV. KINDS OF QUESTIONS

Only rarely is the "essay" question, which you answer in narrative form, used in civil service tests. Civil service tests are usually of the short-answer type. Full instructions for answering these questions will be given to you at the examination. But in case this is your first experience with short-answer questions and separate answer sheets, here is what you need to know:

1) Multiple-choice Questions

Most popular of the short-answer questions is the "multiple choice" or "best answer" question. It can be used, for example, to test for factual knowledge, ability to solve problems or judgment in meeting situations found at work.

A multiple-choice question is normally one of three types—

- It can begin with an incomplete statement followed by several possible endings. You are to find the one ending which *best* completes the statement, although some of the others may not be entirely wrong.
- It can also be a complete statement in the form of a question which is answered by choosing one of the statements listed.
- It can be in the form of a problem – again you select the best answer.

Here is an example of a multiple-choice question with a discussion which should give you some clues as to the method for choosing the right answer:

When an employee has a complaint about his assignment, the action which will *best* help him overcome his difficulty is to
A. discuss his difficulty with his coworkers
B. take the problem to the head of the organization
C. take the problem to the person who gave him the assignment
D. say nothing to anyone about his complaint

In answering this question, you should study each of the choices to find which is best. Consider choice "A" – Certainly an employee may discuss his complaint with fellow employees, but no change or improvement can result, and the complaint remains unresolved. Choice "B" is a poor choice since the head of the organization probably does not know what assignment you have been given, and taking your problem to him is known as "going over the head" of the supervisor. The supervisor, or person who made the assignment, is the person who can clarify it or correct any injustice. Choice "C" is, therefore, correct. To say nothing, as in choice "D," is unwise. Supervisors have and interest in knowing the problems employees are facing, and the employee is seeking a solution to his problem.

2) True/False Questions

The "true/false" or "right/wrong" form of question is sometimes used. Here a complete statement is given. Your job is to decide whether the statement is right or wrong.

SAMPLE: A person-to-person long-distance telephone call costs less than a station-to-station call to the same city.

This statement is wrong, or false, since person-to-person calls are more expensive.

This is not a complete list of all possible question forms, although most of the others are variations of these common types. You will always get complete directions for answering questions. Be sure you understand *how* to mark your answers – ask questions until you do.

V. RECORDING YOUR ANSWERS

For an examination with very few applicants, you may be told to record your answers in the test booklet itself. Separate answer sheets are much more common. If this separate answer sheet is to be scored by machine – and this is often the case – it is highly important that you mark your answers correctly in order to get credit.

An electric scoring machine is often used in civil service offices because of the speed with which papers can be scored. Machine-scored answer sheets must be marked with a pencil, which will be given to you. This pencil has a high graphite content which responds to the electric scoring machine. As a matter of fact, stray dots may register as answers, so do not let your pencil rest on the answer sheet while you are pondering the correct answer. Also, if your pencil lead breaks or is otherwise defective, ask for another.

Since the answer sheet will be dropped in a slot in the scoring machine, be careful not to bend the corners or get the paper crumpled.

The answer sheet normally has five vertical columns of numbers, with 30 numbers to a column. These numbers correspond to the question numbers in your test booklet. After each number, going across the page are four or five pairs of dotted lines. These short dotted lines have small letters or numbers above them. The first two pairs may also have a "T" or "F" above the letters. This indicates that the first two pairs only are to be used if the questions are of the true-false type. If the questions are multiple choice, disregard the "T" and "F" and pay attention only to the small letters or numbers.

Answer your questions in the manner of the sample that follows:

> 32. The largest city in the United States is
>   A. Washington, D.C.
>   B. New York City
>   C. Chicago
>   D. Detroit
>   E. San Francisco

1) Choose the answer you think is best. (New York City is the largest, so "B" is correct.)
2) Find the row of dotted lines numbered the same as the question you are answering. (Find row number 32)
3) Find the pair of dotted lines corresponding to the answer. (Find the pair of lines under the mark "B.")
4) Make a solid black mark between the dotted lines.

VI. BEFORE THE TEST

Common sense will help you find procedures to follow to get ready for an examination. Too many of us, however, overlook these sensible measures. Indeed, nervousness and fatigue have been found to be the most serious reasons why applicants fail to do their best on civil service tests. Here is a list of reminders:

- Begin your preparation early – Don't wait until the last minute to go scurrying around for books and materials or to find out what the position is all about.
- Prepare continuously – An hour a night for a week is better than an all-night cram session. This has been definitely established. What is more, a night a

week for a month will return better dividends than crowding your study into a shorter period of time.

- Locate the place of the exam – You have been sent a notice telling you when and where to report for the examination. If the location is in a different town or otherwise unfamiliar to you, it would be well to inquire the best route and learn something about the building.
- Relax the night before the test – Allow your mind to rest. Do not study at all that night. Plan some mild recreation or diversion; then go to bed early and get a good night's sleep.
- Get up early enough to make a leisurely trip to the place for the test – This way unforeseen events, traffic snarls, unfamiliar buildings, etc. will not upset you.
- Dress comfortably – A written test is not a fashion show. You will be known by number and not by name, so wear something comfortable.
- Leave excess paraphernalia at home – Shopping bags and odd bundles will get in your way. You need bring only the items mentioned in the official notice you received; usually everything you need is provided. Do not bring reference books to the exam. They will only confuse those last minutes and be taken away from you when in the test room.
- Arrive somewhat ahead of time – If because of transportation schedules you must get there very early, bring a newspaper or magazine to take your mind off yourself while waiting.
- Locate the examination room – When you have found the proper room, you will be directed to the seat or part of the room where you will sit. Sometimes you are given a sheet of instructions to read while you are waiting. Do not fill out any forms until you are told to do so; just read them and be prepared.
- Relax and prepare to listen to the instructions
- If you have any physical problem that may keep you from doing your best, be sure to tell the test administrator. If you are sick or in poor health, you really cannot do your best on the exam. You can come back and take the test some other time.

VII. AT THE TEST

The day of the test is here and you have the test booklet in your hand. The temptation to get going is very strong. Caution! There is more to success than knowing the right answers. You must know how to identify your papers and understand variations in the type of short-answer question used in this particular examination. Follow these suggestions for maximum results from your efforts:

1) Cooperate with the monitor
The test administrator has a duty to create a situation in which you can be as much at ease as possible. He will give instructions, tell you when to begin, check to see that you are marking your answer sheet correctly, and so on. He is not there to guard you, although he will see that your competitors do not take unfair advantage. He wants to help you do your best.

2) Listen to all instructions
Don't jump the gun! Wait until you understand all directions. In most civil service tests you get more time than you need to answer the questions. So don't be in a hurry.

Read each word of instructions until you clearly understand the meaning. Study the examples, listen to all announcements and follow directions. Ask questions if you do not understand what to do.

3) Identify your papers

Civil service exams are usually identified by number only. You will be assigned a number; you must not put your name on your test papers. Be sure to copy your number correctly. Since more than one exam may be given, copy your exact examination title.

4) Plan your time

Unless you are told that a test is a "speed" or "rate of work" test, speed itself is usually not important. Time enough to answer all the questions will be provided, but this does not mean that you have all day. An overall time limit has been set. Divide the total time (in minutes) by the number of questions to determine the approximate time you have for each question.

5) Do not linger over difficult questions

If you come across a difficult question, mark it with a paper clip (useful to have along) and come back to it when you have been through the booklet. One caution if you do this – be sure to skip a number on your answer sheet as well. Check often to be sure that you have not lost your place and that you are marking in the row numbered the same as the question you are answering.

6) Read the questions

Be sure you know what the question asks! Many capable people are unsuccessful because they failed to *read* the questions correctly.

7) Answer all questions

Unless you have been instructed that a penalty will be deducted for incorrect answers, it is better to guess than to omit a question.

8) Speed tests

It is often better NOT to guess on speed tests. It has been found that on timed tests people are tempted to spend the last few seconds before time is called in marking answers at random – without even reading them – in the hope of picking up a few extra points. To discourage this practice, the instructions may warn you that your score will be "corrected" for guessing. That is, a penalty will be applied. The incorrect answers will be deducted from the correct ones, or some other penalty formula will be used.

9) Review your answers

If you finish before time is called, go back to the questions you guessed or omitted to give them further thought. Review other answers if you have time.

10) Return your test materials

If you are ready to leave before others have finished or time is called, take ALL your materials to the monitor and leave quietly. Never take any test material with you. The monitor can discover whose papers are not complete, and taking a test booklet may be grounds for disqualification.

VIII. EXAMINATION TECHNIQUES

1) Read the general instructions carefully. These are usually printed on the first page of the exam booklet. As a rule, these instructions refer to the timing of the examination; the fact that you should not start work until the signal and must stop work at a signal, etc. If there are any *special* instructions, such as a choice of questions to be answered, make sure that you note this instruction carefully.

2) When you are ready to start work on the examination, that is as soon as the signal has been given, read the instructions to each question booklet, underline any key words or phrases, such as *least, best, outline, describe* and the like. In this way you will tend to answer as requested rather than discover on reviewing your paper that you *listed without describing*, that you selected the *worst* choice rather than the *best* choice, etc.

3) If the examination is of the objective or multiple-choice type – that is, each question will also give a series of possible answers: A, B, C or D, and you are called upon to select the best answer and write the letter next to that answer on your answer paper – it is advisable to start answering each question in turn. There may be anywhere from 50 to 100 such questions in the three or four hours allotted and you can see how much time would be taken if you read through all the questions before beginning to answer any. Furthermore, if you come across a question or group of questions which you know would be difficult to answer, it would undoubtedly affect your handling of all the other questions.

4) If the examination is of the essay type and contains but a few questions, it is a moot point as to whether you should read all the questions before starting to answer any one. Of course, if you are given a choice – say five out of seven and the like – then it is essential to read all the questions so you can eliminate the two that are most difficult. If, however, you are asked to answer all the questions, there may be danger in trying to answer the easiest one first because you may find that you will spend too much time on it. The best technique is to answer the first question, then proceed to the second, etc.

5) Time your answers. Before the exam begins, write down the time it started, then add the time allowed for the examination and write down the time it must be completed, then divide the time available somewhat as follows:
    - If 3-1/2 hours are allowed, that would be 210 minutes. If you have 80 objective-type questions, that would be an average of 2-1/2 minutes per question. Allow yourself no more than 2 minutes per question, or a total of 160 minutes, which will permit about 50 minutes to review.
    - If for the time allotment of 210 minutes there are 7 essay questions to answer, that would average about 30 minutes a question. Give yourself only 25 minutes per question so that you have about 35 minutes to review.

6) The most important instruction is to *read each question* and make sure you know what is wanted. The second most important instruction is to *time yourself properly* so that you answer every question. The third most

important instruction is to *answer every question*. Guess if you have to but include something for each question. Remember that you will receive no credit for a blank and will probably receive some credit if you write something in answer to an essay question. If you guess a letter – say "B" for a multiple-choice question – you may have guessed right. If you leave a blank as an answer to a multiple-choice question, the examiners may respect your feelings but it will not add a point to your score. Some exams may penalize you for wrong answers, so in such cases *only*, you may not want to guess unless you have some basis for your answer.

7) Suggestions
   a. Objective-type questions
      1. Examine the question booklet for proper sequence of pages and questions
      2. Read all instructions carefully
      3. Skip any question which seems too difficult; return to it after all other questions have been answered
      4. Apportion your time properly; do not spend too much time on any single question or group of questions
      5. Note and underline key words – *all, most, fewest, least, best, worst, same, opposite,* etc.
      6. Pay particular attention to negatives
      7. Note unusual option, e.g., unduly long, short, complex, different or similar in content to the body of the question
      8. Observe the use of "hedging" words – *probably, may, most likely,* etc.
      9. Make sure that your answer is put next to the same number as the question
     10. Do not second-guess unless you have good reason to believe the second answer is definitely more correct
     11. Cross out original answer if you decide another answer is more accurate; do not erase until you are ready to hand your paper in
     12. Answer all questions; guess unless instructed otherwise
     13. Leave time for review

   b. Essay questions
      1. Read each question carefully
      2. Determine exactly what is wanted. Underline key words or phrases.
      3. Decide on outline or paragraph answer
      4. Include many different points and elements unless asked to develop any one or two points or elements
      5. Show impartiality by giving pros and cons unless directed to select one side only
      6. Make and write down any assumptions you find necessary to answer the questions
      7. Watch your English, grammar, punctuation and choice of words
      8. Time your answers; don't crowd material

8) Answering the essay question

Most essay questions can be answered by framing the specific response around several key words or ideas. Here are a few such key words or ideas:

M's: manpower, materials, methods, money, management
P's: purpose, program, policy, plan, procedure, practice, problems, pitfalls, personnel, public relations

a. Six basic steps in handling problems:
1. Preliminary plan and background development
2. Collect information, data and facts
3. Analyze and interpret information, data and facts
4. Analyze and develop solutions as well as make recommendations
5. Prepare report and sell recommendations
6. Install recommendations and follow up effectiveness

b. Pitfalls to avoid
1. *Taking things for granted* – A statement of the situation does not necessarily imply that each of the elements is necessarily true; for example, a complaint may be invalid and biased so that all that can be taken for granted is that a complaint has been registered
2. *Considering only one side of a situation* – Wherever possible, indicate several alternatives and then point out the reasons you selected the best one
3. *Failing to indicate follow up* – Whenever your answer indicates action on your part, make certain that you will take proper follow-up action to see how successful your recommendations, procedures or actions turn out to be
4. *Taking too long in answering any single question* – Remember to time your answers properly

IX. AFTER THE TEST

Scoring procedures differ in detail among civil service jurisdictions although the general principles are the same. Whether the papers are hand-scored or graded by machine we have described, they are nearly always graded by number. That is, the person who marks the paper knows only the number – never the name – of the applicant. Not until all the papers have been graded will they be matched with names. If other tests, such as training and experience or oral interview ratings have been given, scores will be combined. Different parts of the examination usually have different weights. For example, the written test might count 60 percent of the final grade, and a rating of training and experience 40 percent. In many jurisdictions, veterans will have a certain number of points added to their grades.

After the final grade has been determined, the names are placed in grade order and an eligible list is established. There are various methods for resolving ties between those who get the same final grade – probably the most common is to place first the name of the person whose application was received first. Job offers are made from the eligible list in the order the names appear on it. You will be notified of your grade and your rank as soon as all these computations have been made. This will be done as rapidly as possible.

People who are found to meet the requirements in the announcement are called "eligibles." Their names are put on a list of eligible candidates. An eligible's chances of getting a job depend on how high he stands on this list and how fast agencies are filling jobs from the list.

When a job is to be filled from a list of eligibles, the agency asks for the names of people on the list of eligibles for that job. When the civil service commission receives this request, it sends to the agency the names of the three people highest on this list. Or, if the job to be filled has specialized requirements, the office sends the agency the names of the top three persons who meet these requirements from the general list.

The appointing officer makes a choice from among the three people whose names were sent to him. If the selected person accepts the appointment, the names of the others are put back on the list to be considered for future openings.

That is the rule in hiring from all kinds of eligible lists, whether they are for typist, carpenter, chemist, or something else. For every vacancy, the appointing officer has his choice of any one of the top three eligibles on the list. This explains why the person whose name is on top of the list sometimes does not get an appointment when some of the persons lower on the list do. If the appointing officer chooses the second or third eligible, the No. 1 eligible does not get a job at once, but stays on the list until he is appointed or the list is terminated.

X. HOW TO PASS THE INTERVIEW TEST

The examination for which you applied requires an oral interview test. You have already taken the written test and you are now being called for the interview test – the final part of the formal examination.

You may think that it is not possible to prepare for an interview test and that there are no procedures to follow during an interview. Our purpose is to point out some things you can do in advance that will help you and some good rules to follow and pitfalls to avoid while you are being interviewed.

What is an interview supposed to test?

The written examination is designed to test the technical knowledge and competence of the candidate; the oral is designed to evaluate intangible qualities, not readily measured otherwise, and to establish a list showing the relative fitness of each candidate – as measured against his competitors – for the position sought. Scoring is not on the basis of "right" and "wrong," but on a sliding scale of values ranging from "not passable" to "outstanding." As a matter of fact, it is possible to achieve a relatively low score without a single "incorrect" answer because of evident weakness in the qualities being measured.

Occasionally, an examination may consist entirely of an oral test – either an individual or a group oral. In such cases, information is sought concerning the technical knowledges and abilities of the candidate, since there has been no written examination for this purpose. More commonly, however, an oral test is used to supplement a written examination.

Who conducts interviews?

The composition of oral boards varies among different jurisdictions. In nearly all, a representative of the personnel department serves as chairman. One of the members of the board may be a representative of the department in which the candidate would work. In some cases, "outside experts" are used, and, frequently, a businessman or some other representative of the general public is asked to serve. Labor and management or other special groups may be represented. The aim is to secure the services of experts in the appropriate field.

However the board is composed, it is a good idea (and not at all improper or unethical) to ascertain in advance of the interview who the members are and what groups they represent. When you are introduced to them, you will have some idea of their backgrounds and interests, and at least you will not stutter and stammer over their names.

What should be done before the interview?

While knowledge about the board members is useful and takes some of the surprise element out of the interview, there is other preparation which is more substantive. It *is* possible to prepare for an oral interview – in several ways:

1) Keep a copy of your application and review it carefully before the interview

This may be the only document before the oral board, and the starting point of the interview. Know what education and experience you have listed there, and the sequence and dates of all of it. Sometimes the board will ask you to review the highlights of your experience for them; you should not have to hem and haw doing it.

2) Study the class specification and the examination announcement

Usually, the oral board has one or both of these to guide them. The qualities, characteristics or knowledges required by the position sought are stated in these documents. They offer valuable clues as to the nature of the oral interview. For example, if the job involves supervisory responsibilities, the announcement will usually indicate that knowledge of modern supervisory methods and the qualifications of the candidate as a supervisor will be tested. If so, you can expect such questions, frequently in the form of a hypothetical situation which you are expected to solve. NEVER go into an oral without knowledge of the duties and responsibilities of the job you seek.

3) Think through each qualification required

Try to visualize the kind of questions you would ask if you were a board member. How well could you answer them? Try especially to appraise your own knowledge and background in each area, *measured against the job sought*, and identify any areas in which you are weak. Be critical and realistic – do not flatter yourself.

4) Do some general reading in areas in which you feel you may be weak

For example, if the job involves supervision and your past experience has NOT, some general reading in supervisory methods and practices, particularly in the field of human relations, might be useful. Do NOT study agency procedures or detailed manuals. The oral board will be testing your understanding and capacity, not your memory.

5) Get a good night's sleep and watch your general health and mental attitude

You will want a clear head at the interview. Take care of a cold or any other minor ailment, and of course, no hangovers.

What should be done on the day of the interview?

Now comes the day of the interview itself. Give yourself plenty of time to get there. Plan to arrive somewhat ahead of the scheduled time, particularly if your appointment is in the fore part of the day. If a previous candidate fails to appear, the board might be ready for you a bit early. By early afternoon an oral board is almost invariably behind schedule if there are many candidates, and you may have to wait.

Take along a book or magazine to read, or your application to review, but leave any extraneous material in the waiting room when you go in for your interview. In any event, relax and compose yourself.

The matter of dress is important. The board is forming impressions about you – from your experience, your manners, your attitude, and your appearance. Give your personal appearance careful attention. Dress your best, but not your flashiest. Choose conservative, appropriate clothing, and be sure it is immaculate. This is a business interview, and your appearance should indicate that you regard it as such. Besides, being well groomed and properly dressed will help boost your confidence.

Sooner or later, someone will call your name and escort you into the interview room. *This is it.* From here on you are on your own. It is too late for any more preparation. But remember, you asked for this opportunity to prove your fitness, and you are here because your request was granted.

What happens when you go in?

The usual sequence of events will be as follows: The clerk (who is often the board stenographer) will introduce you to the chairman of the oral board, who will introduce you to the other members of the board. Acknowledge the introductions before you sit down. Do not be surprised if you find a microphone facing you or a stenotypist sitting by. Oral interviews are usually recorded in the event of an appeal or other review.

Usually the chairman of the board will open the interview by reviewing the highlights of your education and work experience from your application – primarily for the benefit of the other members of the board, as well as to get the material into the record. Do not interrupt or comment unless there is an error or significant misinterpretation; if that is the case, do not hesitate. But do not quibble about insignificant matters. Also, he will usually ask you some question about your education, experience or your present job – partly to get you to start talking and to establish the interviewing "rapport." He may start the actual questioning, or turn it over to one of the other members. Frequently, each member undertakes the questioning on a particular area, one in which he is perhaps most competent, so you can expect each member to participate in the examination. Because time is limited, you may also expect some rather abrupt switches in the direction the questioning takes, so do not be upset by it. Normally, a board member will not pursue a single line of questioning unless he discovers a particular strength or weakness.

After each member has participated, the chairman will usually ask whether any member has any further questions, then will ask you if you have anything you wish to add. Unless you are expecting this question, it may floor you. Worse, it may start you off on an extended, extemporaneous speech. The board is not usually seeking more information. The question is principally to offer you a last opportunity to present further qualifications or to indicate that you have nothing to add. So, if you feel that a significant qualification or characteristic has been overlooked, it is proper to point it out in a sentence or so. Do not compliment the board on the thoroughness of their examination – they have been sketchy, and you know it. If you wish, merely say, "No thank you, I have nothing further to add." This is a point where you can "talk yourself out" of a good impression or fail to present an important bit of information. Remember, *you close the interview yourself.*

The chairman will then say, "That is all, Mr. _____, thank you." Do not be startled; the interview is over, and quicker than you think. Thank him, gather your belongings and take your leave. Save your sigh of relief for the other side of the door.

How to put your best foot forward

Throughout this entire process, you may feel that the board individually and collectively is trying to pierce your defenses, seek out your hidden weaknesses and embarrass and confuse you. Actually, this is not true. They are obliged to make an appraisal of your qualifications for the job you are seeking, and they want to see you in your best light. Remember, they must interview all candidates and a non-cooperative candidate may become a failure in spite of their best efforts to bring out his qualifications. Here are 15 suggestions that will help you:

1) Be natural – Keep your attitude confident, not cocky

If you are not confident that you can do the job, do not expect the board to be. Do not apologize for your weaknesses, try to bring out your strong points. The board is interested in a positive, not negative, presentation. Cockiness will antagonize any board member and make him wonder if you are covering up a weakness by a false show of strength.

2) Get comfortable, but don't lounge or sprawl

Sit erectly but not stiffly. A careless posture may lead the board to conclude that you are careless in other things, or at least that you are not impressed by the importance of the occasion. Either conclusion is natural, even if incorrect. Do not fuss with your clothing, a pencil or an ashtray. Your hands may occasionally be useful to emphasize a point; do not let them become a point of distraction.

3) Do not wisecrack or make small talk

This is a serious situation, and your attitude should show that you consider it as such. Further, the time of the board is limited – they do not want to waste it, and neither should you.

4) Do not exaggerate your experience or abilities

In the first place, from information in the application or other interviews and sources, the board may know more about you than you think. Secondly, you probably will not get away with it. An experienced board is rather adept at spotting such a situation, so do not take the chance.

5) If you know a board member, do not make a point of it, yet do not hide it

Certainly you are not fooling him, and probably not the other members of the board. Do not try to take advantage of your acquaintanceship – it will probably do you little good.

6) Do not dominate the interview

Let the board do that. They will give you the clues – do not assume that you have to do all the talking. Realize that the board has a number of questions to ask you, and do not try to take up all the interview time by showing off your extensive knowledge of the answer to the first one.

7) Be attentive

You only have 20 minutes or so, and you should keep your attention at its sharpest throughout. When a member is addressing a problem or question to you, give him your undivided attention. Address your reply principally to him, but do not exclude the other board members.

8) Do not interrupt

A board member may be stating a problem for you to analyze. He will ask you a question when the time comes. Let him state the problem, and wait for the question.

9) Make sure you understand the question

Do not try to answer until you are sure what the question is. If it is not clear, restate it in your own words or ask the board member to clarify it for you. However, do not haggle about minor elements.

10) Reply promptly but not hastily

A common entry on oral board rating sheets is "candidate responded readily," or "candidate hesitated in replies." Respond as promptly and quickly as you can, but do not jump to a hasty, ill-considered answer.

11) Do not be peremptory in your answers

A brief answer is proper – but do not fire your answer back. That is a losing game from your point of view. The board member can probably ask questions much faster than you can answer them.

12) Do not try to create the answer you think the board member wants

He is interested in what kind of mind you have and how it works – not in playing games. Furthermore, he can usually spot this practice and will actually grade you down on it.

13) Do not switch sides in your reply merely to agree with a board member

Frequently, a member will take a contrary position merely to draw you out and to see if you are willing and able to defend your point of view. Do not start a debate, yet do not surrender a good position. If a position is worth taking, it is worth defending.

14) Do not be afraid to admit an error in judgment if you are shown to be wrong

The board knows that you are forced to reply without any opportunity for careful consideration. Your answer may be demonstrably wrong. If so, admit it and get on with the interview.

15) Do not dwell at length on your present job

The opening question may relate to your present assignment. Answer the question but do not go into an extended discussion. You are being examined for a *new* job, not your present one. As a matter of fact, try to phrase ALL your answers in terms of the job for which you are being examined.

Basis of Rating

Probably you will forget most of these "do's" and "don'ts" when you walk into the oral interview room. Even remembering them all will not ensure you a passing grade. Perhaps you did not have the qualifications in the first place. But remembering them will help you to put your best foot forward, without treading on the toes of the board members.

Rumor and popular opinion to the contrary notwithstanding, an oral board wants you to make the best appearance possible. They know you are under pressure – but they also want to see how you respond to it as a guide to what your reaction would be under the pressures of the job you seek. They will be influenced by the degree of poise you display, the personal traits you show and the manner in which you respond.

EXAMINATION SECTION

TEST 1

DIRECTIONS:
   Each question or incomplete statement is followed by several suggested answers or completions. Select the one that *BEST* answers the
question or completes the statement. *PRINT THE LETTER OF THE CORRECT
ANSWER IN THE SPACE AT THE RIGHT.*

Questions 1-5.
DIRECTIONS: Questions 1 through 5 consist of sentences each of which
contains one underlined word whose meaning you are to identify by
marking your answer either A, B, C, or D.
                          EXAMPLE
   Public employees should avoid <u>unethical</u> conduct.
   The word *unethical,* as used in the sentence, means, most nearly,
      A. fine   B. dishonest C. polite   D. sleepy
   The correct answer is dishonest (B). Therefore, you should mark
your answer B.

1. Employees who can produce a <u>considerable</u> amount of good   1. ...
   work are very valuable.
   The word *considerable,* as used in the sentence, means,
   most nearly,
      A. large   B. potential C. necessary D. frequent
2. No person should <u>assume</u> that he knows more than anyone   2. ...
   else.
   The word *assume,* as used in the sentence, means, most nearly,
      A. verify   B. hope   C. suppose   D. argue
3. The parties decided to <u>negotiate</u> through the night.   3. ...
   The word *negotiate,* as used in the sentence, means, most
   nearly,
      A. suffer   B. play   C. think   D. bargain
4. Employees who have <u>severe</u> emotional problems may create   4. ...
   problems at work.
   The word *severe,* as used in the sentence, means, most nearly,
      A. serious   B. surprising C. several   D. common
5. Supervisors should try to be as <u>objective</u> as possible   5. ...
   when dealing with subordinates.
   The word *objective,* as used in the sentence, means, most
   nearly,
      A. pleasant   B. courteous C. fair   D. strict

Questions 6-10.
DIRECTIONS: In each of Questions 6 through 10, *one* word is wrongly
used because it is *NOT* in keeping with the intended meaning of the
statement. First, decide which word is wrongly used; then select
as your answer the right word which really belongs in its place.
                          EXAMPLE
   The employee told ill and requested permission to leave early.
      A. felt   B. considered C. cried   D. spoke
The word "told" is clearly wrong and not in keeping with the intended
meaning of the quotation.
   The word "felt" (A), however, would clearly convey the intended
meaning of the sentence. Option A is correct. Your answer space,
therefore, would be marked A.

6. Only unwise supervisors would deliberately overload their 6. ...
   subordinates in order to create themselves look good.
      A. delegate   B. make   C. reduce   D. produce

7. In a democratic organization each employee is seen as a 7. ...
   special individual kind of fair treatment.
      A. granted   B. denial   C. perhaps   D. deserving

8. In order to function the work flow in an office you should 8. ...
   begin by identifying each important procedure being performed in that office.
      A. uniformity B. study   C. standards D. reward

9. A wise supervisor tries to save employees' time by 9. ...
   simplifying forms or adding forms where possible.
      A. taxing B. supervising C. eliminating D. protecting

10. A public agency, whenever it changes its program, should 10. ...
    give requirements to the need for retraining its employees.
       A. legislation B. consideration C. permission D. advice

Questions 11-15.

DIRECTIONS: Answer each of Questions 11 through 15 *ONLY* on the basis
of the reading passage preceding each question.

11. Things may not always be what they seem to be. Thus, 11. ...
    the wise supervisor should analyze his problems and
    determine whether there is something there that does not
    meet the eye. For example, what may seem on the surface
    to be a personality clash between two subordinates may
    really be a problem of faulty organization, bad communi-
    cation, or bad scheduling.
    Which one of the following statements *BEST* supports this
    passage?
       A. The wise supervisor should avoid personality clashes.
       B. The smart supervisor should figure out what really is
          going on.
       C. Bad scheduling is the result of faulty organization.
       D. The best supervisor is the one who communicates ef-
          fectively.

12. Some supervisors, under the pressure of meeting dead- 12. ...
    lines, become harsh and dictatorial to their subordinates.
    However, the supervisor most likely to be effective in
    meeting deadlines is one who absorbs or cushions pressures
    from above.
    According to the passage, if a supervisor wishes to meet
    deadlines, it is *MOST* important that he
       A. be informative to his superiors
       B. encourage personal initiative among his subordinates
       C. become harsh and dictatorial to his subordinates
       D. protects his subordinates from pressures from above

13. When giving instructions, a supervisor must always make 13. ...
    clear his meaning, leaving no room for misunderstanding.
    For example, a supervisor who tells a subordinate to do a
    task "as soon as possible" might legitimately be under-
    stood to mean either "it's top priority" or "do it when
    you can."
    Which of the following statements is *BEST* supported by the
    passage?
       A. Subordinates will attempt to avoid work by deliberate-
          ly distorting instructions.

    B. Instructions should be short, since brief instruc-
       tions are the clearest.

    C. Less educated subordinates are more likely to honest-
       ly misunderstand instructions.

    D. A supervisor should give precise instructions that
       cannot be misinterpreted.

14. Practical formulas are often suggested to simplify what   14. ...
    a supervisor should know and how he should behave, such
    as the four F's (be firm, fair, friendly, and factual).
    But such simple formulas are really broad principles, not
    necessarily specific guides in a real situation.
    According to the passage, simple formulas for supervisory
    behavior

    A. are superior to complicated theories and principles

    B. not always of practical use in actual situations

    C. useful only if they are fair and factual

    D. would be better understood if written in clear
       language

15. Many management decisions are made far removed from the   15. ...
    actual place of operations. Therefore, there is a great
    need for reliable reports and records and, the larger the
    organization, the greater is the need for such reports and
    records.
    According to the passage, management decisions made far
    from the place of operations are

    A. dependent to a great extent on reliable reports and
       records

    B. sometimes in error because of the great distances
       involved

    C. generally unreliable because of poor communications

    D. generally more accurate than on-the-scene decisions

16. Assume that you have just been advanced to a supervisory   16. ...
    administrative position and have been assigned as super-
    visor to a new office with subordinates you do not know.
    The *BEST* way for you to establish good relations with these
    new subordinates would be to

    A. announce that all actions of the previous supervisor
       are now cancelled

    B. hold a meeting and warn them that you will not tolerate
       loafing on the job

    C. reassign all your subordinates to new tasks on the
       theory that a thorough shake-up is good for morale

    D. act fairly and show helpful interest in their work

17. One of your subordinates asks you to let her arrive at   17. ...
    work 15 minutes later than usual but leave for the day
    15 minutes later than she usually does. This is temporarily
    necessary, your subordinate states, because of early morning
    medication she must give her sick child.
    Which of the following would be the *MOST* appropriate action
    for you to take?

    A. *Suggest* to your subordinate that she choose another
       family doctor

    B. *Warn* your subordinate that untruthful excuses are not
       acceptable

C. *Tell* your subordinate that you will consider the request and let her know very shortly
D. *Deny* the request since late arrival at work inter-
   feres with work performance

18. A young newly-hired employee asked his supervisor several   18. ...
    times for advice on private financial matters. The super-
    visor commented, in a friendly manner, that he considered
    it undesirable to give such advice.
    The supervisor's response was
    A. *unwise;* the supervisor missed an opportunity to ad-
       vise the employee on an important matter
    B. *wise;* if the financial advice was wrong, it could
       damage the supervisor's relationship with the sub-
       ordinate
    C. *unwise;* the subordinate will take up the matter with
       his fellow workers and probably get poor advice
    D. *wise;* the supervisor should never advise subordinates
       on any matter

19. *Which* of the following is the *MOST* justified reason for   19. ...
    a supervisor to pay any serious attention to a subordinate's
    off-the-job behavior? The
    A. subordinate's life style is different from the super-
       visor's way of life
    B. subordinate has become well-known as a serious painter
       of fine art
    C. subordinate's work has become very poor as a result of
       his or her personal problems
    D. subordinate is a reserved person who, at work, seldom
       speaks of personal matters

20. One of your subordinates complains to you that you assign   20. ...
    him to the least pleasant jobs more often than anyone else.
    You are disturbed by this complaint since you believe
    you have always rotated such assignments on a fair basis.
    Of the following, it would be *BEST* for you to tell the
    complaining subordinate that
    A. you will review your past assignment records and
       discuss the matter with him further
    B. complaints to supervisors are not the wise way to
       get ahead on the job
    C. disciplinary action will follow if the complaint is
       not justified
    D. he may be correct, but you do not have sufficient
       time to verify the complaint

21. Assume that you have called one of your subordinates into   21. ...
    your office to talk about the increasing number of care-
    less errors in her work. Until recently, this subordinate
    had been doing good work, but this is no longer so. Your
    subordinate does not seem to respond to your questions about
    the reason for her poor work.
    In these circumstances, your *next* step should be to tell her
    A. that her continued silence will result in severe
       disciplinary action
    B. to request an immediate transfer from your unit
    C. to return when she is ready to respond
    D. to be more open with you so that her work problem
       can be identified

4

22. Assume that you are given a complicated assignment with 22. ...
a tight deadline set by your superior. Shortly after you
begin work you realize that, if you are to do a top quality
job, you cannot possibly meet the deadline.
In these circumstances, what should be your *FIRST* course of
action?
   A. *Continue* working as rapidly as possible, hoping that
   you will meet the deadline after all
   B. *Request* the assignment be given to an employee whom
   you believe works faster
   C. *Advise* your superior of the problem and see whether
   the deadline can be extended
   D. *Advise* your superior that the deadline cannot be met
   and, therefore, you will not start the job

23. Assume that a member of the public comes to you to com- 23. ...
plain about a long-standing practice of your agency.
The complaint seems to be justified.
Which one of the following is the *BEST* way for you to
handle this situation?
   A. *Inform* the complainant that you will have the agency
   practice looked into and that he will be advised of
   any action taken
   B. *Listen* politely, express sympathy, and state that
   you see no fault in the practice
   C. *Express* agreement with the practice on the ground
   that it has been in effect for many years
   D. *Advise* the complainant that things will work out well
   in good time

24. One of your subordinates tells you that he sees no good 24. ...
reason for having departmental safety rules.
Which one of the following replies would be *BEST* for you
to make?
   A. Rules are meant to be obeyed without question.
   B. All types of rules are equally important.
   C. Safety rules are meant to protect people from injury.
   D. If a person is careful enough, he doesn't have to ob-
   serve safety rules.

25. Assume that a supervisor, when he issues instructions to 25. ...
his subordinates, usually names his superior as the source
of these instructions.
This practice is, generally,
   A. *wise,* since if things go wrong, the subordinates will
   know whom to blame
   B. *unwise,* since it may give the subordinates the impression that the supervisor doesn't really support the
   instructions
   C. *wise,* since it clearly invites the subordinates to go
   to higher authority if they don't like the instructions
   D. *unwise,* since the subordinates may thereby be given
   too much information

KEY (CORRECT ANSWERS)

1. A		11. B	
2. C		12. D	
3. D		13. D	
4. A		14. B	
5. C		15. A	
6. B		16. D	
7. D		17. C	
8. B		18. B	
9. C		19. C	
10. B		20. A	

21. D
22. C
23. A
24. C
25. B

———

TEST 2

DIRECTIONS:

Each question or incomplete statement is followed by several suggested answers or completions. Select the one that *BEST* answers the question or completes the statement. *PRINT THE LETTER OF THE CORRECT ANSWER IN THE SPACE AT THE RIGHT.*

1. An office aide is assigned as a receptionist in a busy office. The office aide often has stretches of idle time between visitors.
   In this situation, the supervisor should
   A. *give* the receptionist non-urgent clerical jobs which can quickly be done at the reception desk
   B. *offer* all office aides an opportunity to volunteer for this assignment
   C. *eliminate* the receptionist assignment
   D. *continue* the arrangement unchanged, because receptionist duties are so important nothing should interfere with them

   1. ...

2. A supervisor can *MOST* correctly assume that an employee is not performing up to his usual standard when the employee does not handle a task as skillfully as
   A. do other employees who have received less training
   B. do similar employees having comparable work experience
   C. he has handled it in several recent instances
   D. the supervisor himself could handle it

   2. ...

3. Assume that you receive a suggestion that you direct all the typists in a typing pool to complete the identical quantity of work each day.
   For you to adopt this suggestion would be
   A. *advisable;* it will demonstrate the absence of supervisory favoritism
   B. *advisable;* all employees in a given title should be treated identically
   C. *inadvisable;* a supervisor should decide on work standards without interference from others
   D. *inadvisable;* it ignores variations in specific assignments and individual skills

   3. ...

4. A certain supervisor encouraged her subordinates to tell her if they become aware of possible job problems.
   This practice is *good MAINLY* because
   A. early awareness of job problems allows more time for seeking solutions
   B. such expected job problems may not develop
   C. the supervisor will be able to solve the job problem without consulting other people
   D. the supervisor will be able to place responsibility for poor work

   4. ...

5. Some supervisors will discuss with a subordinate how he is doing on the job only when indicating his mistakes or faults.
   Which of the following is the *MOST* likely result of such a practice?
   A. The subordinate will become discouraged and frustrated.

   5. ...

B. Management will set work standards too low.

C. The subordinate will be favorably impressed by the supervisor's frankness.

D. Supervisors will avoid creating any impression of favoritism.

6. A supervisor calls in a subordinate he supervises to discuss the subordinate's annual work performance, indicating his work deficiencies and also praising his job strengths. The subordinate nods his head as if in agreement with his supervisor's comments on both his strengths and weaknesses, but actually says nothing, even after the supervisor has completed his comments. At this point, the supervisor should

   6. ...

A. end the session and assume that the subordinate agrees completely with the evaluation

B. end the session, since all the subordinate's good and bad points have been identified

C. ask the subordinate whether the criticism is justified, and, if so, what he, the supervisor, can do to help

D. thank the subordinate for being so fair-minded in accepting the criticism in a positive manner

7. The successful supervisor is often one who gives serious attention to his subordinates' needs for job satisfaction. A supervisor who believes this statement is *MOST* likely to

   7. ...

A. treat all subordinates in an identical manner, irrespective of individual differences

B. permit each subordinate to perform his work as he wishes, within reasonable limits

C. give all subordinates both criticism and praise in equal measure

D. provide each subordinate with as much direct supervision as possible

8. Assume that you are supervising seven subordinates and have been asked by your superior to prepare an especially complex report due today. Its completion will take the rest of the day. You break down the assignment into simple parts and give a different part to each subordinate. If you were to explain the work of each subordinate to more than one subordinate, your decision would be

   8. ...

A. *wise;* this would prevent boredom

B. *unwise;* valuable time would be lost

C. *wise;* your subordinates would become well-rounded

D. *unwise;* your subordinates would lose their competitive spirit

9. Suppose that an office associate whom you supervise has given you a well-researched report on a problem in an area in which he is expert. However, the report lacks solutions or recommendations. You know this office associate to be fearful of stating his opinions. In these circumstances, you should tell him that

   9. ...

A. you will seek recommendations on the problem from other, even if less expert, office associates

B. his work is unsatisfactory, in hope of arousing him to greater assertiveness

C. you need his advise and expertise to help you reach
   a decision on the problem
D. his uncooperative behavior leaves you no choice but
   to speak to your superior

10. If a supervisor wishes to have the work of his unit com-   10. ...
    pleted on schedule, it is usually *MOST* important to
    A. avoid listening to employees' complaints, thereby
       discouraging dissatisfaction
    B. perform much of the work himself, since he is general-
       ly more capable
    C. observe employees continuously, so they do not slacken
       their efforts
    D. set up the work carefully, then stay informed as to
       how it is moving

11. Of the following agencies, the one *MOST* likely to work   11. ...
    out a proposed budget close to its real needs is
    A. a newly-created agency staffed by inexperienced ad-
       ministrators
    B. funded with a considerable amount of money
    C. an existing agency which intends to install new,
       experimental systems for doing its work
    D. an existing agency which can base its estimate on
       its experience during the past few years

12. Assume that you are asked to prepare a report on the ex-   12. ...
    pected costs and benefits of a proposed new program to be
    installed in your office. However, you are aware that
    certain factors are not really measurable in dollars and
    cents.
    As a result, you should
    A. *identify* the non-measurable factors and state why
       they are important
    B. *assign* a fixed money value to all factors that are
       not really measurable
    C. *recommend* that programs containing non-measurable
       factors should be dropped
    D. *assume* that the non-measurable factors are really
       unimportant

13. Assume that you are asked for your opinion as to the   13. ...
    necessity for hiring more employees to perform certain
    revenue-producing work in your office.
    The information that you will *MOST* likely need in giving
    an informed opinion is
    A. whether public opinion would favor hiring additional
       employees
    B. an estimate of the probable additional revenue com-
       pared with the additional personnel costs
    C. the total cots of all city operations in contrast to
       all city revenues
    D. the method by which present employees would be selected
       for promotion in an expanded operation

14. The *most* reasonable number of subordinates for a super-   14. ...
    visor to have is *BEST* determined by the
    A. average number of subordinates other supervisors have
    B. particular responsibilities given to the supervisor

    C. supervisor's educational background

    D. personalities of the subordinates assigned to the
       supervisor

15. Most subordinates would need less supervision if they   15. ...
knew what they were supposed to do.
An *ESSENTIAL first* step in fixing in subordinates' minds
exactly what is required of them is to

    A. *require* that supervisors be firm in their supervision
      of subordinates

    B. *encourage* subordinates to determine their own work
      standards

    C. *encourage* subordinates to submit suggestions to im-
      prove procedures

    D. *standardize* and simplify procedures and logically
      schedule activities

16. Assume that you have been asked to recommend an appro-   16. ...
priate office layout to correspond with a just completed
office reorganization.
Which of the following is it *MOST* advisable to recommend?

    A. *Allocate* most of the space for traffic flow

    B. *Use* the center area only for traffic flow

    C. *Situate* close to each other those units whose work is
      closely related

    D. *Group* in an out-of-the-way corner the supply and file
      cabinets

17. Although an organization chart will illustrate the formal 17. ...
structure of an agency, it will seldom show a true picture
of its actual workings.
Which of the following *BEST* explains this statement?
Organization charts

    A. are often prepared by employees who may   exaggerate
      their own importance

    B. usually show titles and sometimes names rather than
      the actual contacts and movements between employees

    C. are likely to discourage the use of official titles,
      and in so doing promote greater freedom in human re-
      lations

    D. usually show the informal arrangements and dealings
      between employees

18. Assume that a supervisor of a large unit has a variety   18. ...
of tasks to perform, and that he gives each of his subordinates just one set of tasks to do. He never rotates
subordinates from one set of tasks to another.
Which one of the following is the *MOST* likely *advantage*
to be gained by this practice?

    A. Each subordinate will get to know all the tasks of
      the unit.

    B. The subordinate will be encouraged to learn all they
      can about all the unit's tasks.

    C. Each subordinate will become an expert in his par-
      ticular set of tasks.

    D. The subordinates will improve their opportunities
      for promotion.

19. Listed below are four steps commonly used in trying to   19. ...
solve administrative problems. These four steps are not
listed in the order in which they normally would be taken.
If they were listed in the proper order, which step should
be taken *FIRST*?
   I. Choosing the most practical solution to the problem
  II. Analyzing the essential facts about the problem
 III. Correctly identifying the problem
  IV. Following up to see if the solution chosen really works
The *CORRECT* answer is:
  A. III   B. I   C. II   D. IV

20. Assume that another agency informally tells you that   20. ...
most of your agency's reports are coming to them with
careless errors made by many of your office aides.
Which one of the following is *MOST* likely to solve this
problem?
  A. *Require* careful review of all outgoing reports by the
     supervisors of the office aides
  B. *Request* the other agency to make necessary corrections
     whenever such errors come to their attention
  C. *Ask* the other agency to submit a written report on
     this situation
  D. *Establish* a small unit to review all reports received
     from other agencies

21. Assume that you supervise an office which gets two kinds   21. ...
of work. One kind is high-priority and must be done within
two days. The other kind of work must be done within two
weeks.
Which one of the following instructions would be *MOST* rea-
sonable for you to give to your subordinates in this office?
  A. If a backlog builds up during the day, clean the back-
     log up first, regardless of priority
  B. Spend half the day doing priority work and the other
     half doing non-priority work
  C. Generally do the priority work first as soon as it
     is received
  D. Usually do the work in the order in which it comes
     in, priority or non-priority

22. An experienced supervisor should do advance planning of   22. ...
his subordinates' work assignments and schedules.
Which one of the following is the *BEST* reason for such
advance planning? It
  A. enables the supervisor to do less supervision
  B. will assure the assignment of varied duties
  C. will make certain a high degree of discipline
     among subordinates
  D. helps make certain that essential operations are
     adequately covered

23. Agencies are required to evaluate the performance of   23. ...
their employees.
Which one of the following would generally be *POOR*
evaluation practice by an agency rater? The rater
  A. regularly observes the performance of the employee
     being rated

B. in evaluating the employee, acquaints himself
   with the employee's job
C. uses objective standards in evaluating the employee
   being rated
D. uses different standards in evaluating men and women

24. A good supervisor should have a clear idea of the quanti- 24. ...
    ty and quality of his subordinates' work.
    Which one of the following sources would normally provide
    a supervisor with the *LEAST* reliable information about a
    subordinate's work performance?
    A. Discussion with a friend of the subordinate
    B. Comments by other supervisors who have worked recently
       with the subordinate
    C. Opinions of fellow workers who work closely with the
       subordinate on a daily basis
    D. Comparison with work records of others doing similar
       work during the same period of time

25. In order to handle the ordinary work of an office, a   25. ...
    supervisor sets up standard work procedures.
    The *MOST* likely benefit of this is to reduce the need
    to
    A. motivate employees to do superior work
    B. rethink what has to be done every time a routine
       matter comes up
    C. keep records and write reports
    D. change work procedures as new situations come up

KEY (CORRECT ANSWERS)

1. A		11. D	
2. C		12. A	
3. D		13. B	
4. A		14. B	
5. A		15. D	
6. C		16. C	
7. B		17. B	
8. B		18. C	
9. C		19. A	
10. D		20. A	

21. C
22. D
23. D
24. A
25. B

EXAMINATION SECTION
TEST 1

DIRECTIONS: Each question or incomplete statement is followed by several suggested answers or completions. Select the one that BEST answers the question or completes the statement. *PRINT THE LETTER OF THE CORRECT ANSWER IN THE SPACE AT THE RIGHT.*

1. In almost every organization, there is a nucleus of highly important functions commonly designated as *management*. Which of the following statements BEST characterizes *management*?
    A. Getting things done through others
    B. The highest level of intelligence in any organization
    C. The process whereby democratic and participative activities are maximized
    D. The *first among equals*

1.____

2. Strategies in problem-solving are important to anyone aspiring to advancement in the field of administration. Which of the following is BEST classified as the first step in the process of problem-solving?
    A. Collection and organization of data
    B. The formulation of a plan
    C. The definition of the problem
    D. The development of a method and methodology

2.____

3. One of the objectives of preparing a budget is to
    A. create optimistic goals which each department can attempt to meet
    B. create an overall company goal by combining the budgets of the various departments
    C. be able to compare planned expenditures against actual expenditures
    D. be able to identify accounting errors

3.____

4. The rise in demand for *systems* personnel in industrial and governmental organizations over the past five years has been extraordinary.
    In which of the following areas would a *systems* specialist assigned to an agency be LEAST likely to be of assistance?
    A. Developing, recommending, and establishing an effective cost and inventory system
    B. Development and maintenance of training manuals
    C. Reviewing existing work procedures and recommending improvements
    D. Development of aptitude tests for new employees

4.____

5. Management experts have come to the conclusion that the traditional forms of motivation used in industry and government, which emphasize authority over and economic rewards for the employee, are no longer appropriate.

5.____

To which of the following factors do such experts
attribute the GREATEST importance in producing this change?
  A. The desire of employees to satisfy material needs
     has become greater and more complex.
  B. The desire for social satisfaction has become the
     most important aspect of the job for the average
     worker.
  C. With greater standardization of work processes, there
     has been an increase in the willingness of workers
     to accept discipline.
  D. In general, employee organizations have made it more
     difficult for management to fire an employee.

6. In preparing a budget, it is usually considered advisable   6.___
   to start the initial phases of preparation at the operational level of management.
   Of the following, the justification that management experts
   usually advance as MOST reasonable for this practice is
   that operating managers, as a consequence of their involve-
   ment, will
  A. develop a background in finance or accounting
  B. have an understanding of the organizational structure
  C. tend to feel responsible for carrying out budget
     objectives
  D. have the ability to see the overall financial picture

7. An administrative officer has been asked by his superior   7.___
   to write a concise, factual report with objective conclu-
   sions and recommendations based on facts assembled by
   other researchers.
   Of the following factors, the administrative officer should
   give LEAST consideration to
  A. the educational level of the person or persons for
     whom the report is being prepared
  B. the use to be made of the report
  C. the complexity of the problem
  D. his own feelings about the importance of the problem

8. In an agency, upon which of the following is a supervisor's   8.___
   effectiveness MOST likely to depend?
   The
  A. degree to which a supervisor allows subordinates to
     participate in the decision-making process and the
     setting of objectives
  B. degree to which a supervisor's style meets management's
     objectives and subordinates' needs
  C. strength and forcefulness of the supervisor in
     pursuing his objectives
  D. expertise and knowledge the supervisor has about the
     specific work to be done

9. For authority to be effective, which of the following is   9.___
   the MOST basic requirement?
   Authority must be
     A. absolute   B. formalized   C. accepted   D. delegated

10. Management no longer abhors the idea of employees taking
    daily work breaks, but prefers to schedule such breaks
    rather than to allot to each employee a standard amount
    of free time to be taken off during the day as he wishes.
    Which of the following BEST expresses the reason management
    theorists give for the practice of scheduling such breaks?
    A. Many jobs fall into natural work units which are
       scheduled, and the natural time to take a break is
       at the end of the unit.
    B. Taking a scheduled break permits socialization and a
       feeling of accomplishment.
    C. Managers have concluded that scheduling rest periods
       seems to reduce the incidence of unscheduled ones.
    D. Many office workers who really need such breaks are
       hesitant about taking them unless they are scheduled.

10.___

11. The computer represents one of the major developments of
    modern technology. It is widely used in both scientific
    and managerial activities because of its many advantages.
    Which of the following is NOT an advantage gained by
    management in the use of the computer?
    A computer
    A. provides the manager with a greatly enlarged memory
       so that he can easily be provided with data for
       decision making
    B. relieves the manager of basic decision-making respon-
       sibility, thereby giving him more time for directing
       and controlling
    C. performs routine, repetitive calculations with greater
       precision and reliability than employees
    D. provides a capacity for rapid simulations of alterna-
       tive solutions to problem solving

11.___

12. A supervisor of a unit in a division is usually respon-
    sible for all of the following EXCEPT
    A. the conduct of subordinates in the achievement of
       division objectives
    B. maintaining quality standards in the unit
    C. the protection and care of materials and equipment
       in the unit
    D. performing the most detailed tasks in the unit himself

12.___

13. You have been assigned to teach a new employee the func-
    tions and procedures of your office.
    In your introductory talk, which of the following approaches
    is PREFERABLE?
    A. Advise the new employee of the employee benefits and
       services available to him, over and above his salary.
    B. Discuss honestly the negative aspects of departmental
       procedures and indicate methods available to overcome
       them.
    C. Give the new employee an understanding of the general
       purpose of office procedures and functions and of their
       relevance to departmental objectives
    D. Give a basic and detailed explanation of the operations
       of your office, covering all functions and procedures

13.___

14. It is your responsibility to assign work to several   14.___
    clerks under your supervision. One of the clerks indig-
    nantly refuses to accept an assignment and asks to be
    given something else. He has not yet indicated why he
    does not want the assignment, but is sitting there glaring
    at you, awaiting your reaction.
    Of the following, which is the FIRST action you should take?
       A. Ask the employee into your office in order to reprimand
          him and tell him emphatically that he must accept the
          assignment.
       B. Talk to the employee privately in an effort to find the
          reason for his indignation and refusal, and then base
          your action upon your findings.
       C. Let the matter drop for a day or two to allow the
          employee to cool off before you insist that he accept
          the assignment.
       D. Inform the employee quietly and calmly that as his
          supervisor you have selected him for this assignment
          and that you fully expect him to accept it.

15. Administrative officers are expected to be able to handle   15.___
    duties delegated to them by their supervisors and to be
    able, as they advance in status, to delegate tasks to
    assistants.
    When considering whether to delegate tasks to a subordinate,
    which of the following questions should be LEAST important
    to an administrative officer?
    In the delegated tasks,
       A. how significant are the decisions to be made, and how
          much consultation will be involved?
       B. to what extent is uniformity and close coordination
          of activity required?
       C. to what extent must speedy-on-the-spot decisions be
          made?
       D. to what extent will delegation relieve the administra-
          tive officer of his burden of responsibility?

16. A functional forms file is a collection of forms which   16.___
    are grouped by
       A. purpose   B. department   C. title   D. subject

17. All of the following are reasons to consult a records   17.___
    retention schedule except one.
    Which one is that?
    To determine
       A. whether something should be filed
       B. how long something should stay in file
       C. who should be assigned to filing
       D. when something on file should be destroyed

18. Listed below are four of the steps in the process of pre-   18.___
    paring correspondence for filing.
    If they were to be put in logical sequence, the SECOND
    step would be
       A. preparing cross-reference sheets or cards
       B. coding the correspondence using a classification system

    C. sorting the correspondence in the order to be filed
    D. checking for follow-up action required and preparing
       a follow-up slip

19. New material added to a file folder should USUALLY be   19.____
    inserted
       A. in the order of importance (the most important in front)
       B. in the order of importance (the most important in back)
       C. chronologically (most recent in front)
       D. chronologically (most recent in back)

20. An individual is looking for a name in the white pages of   20.____
    a telephone directory.
    Which of the following BEST describes the system of filing
    found there?
    A(n)_____ file
       A. alphabetic   B. sequential
       C. locator   D. index

21. The MAIN purpose of a tickler file is to   21.____
       A. help prevent overlooking matters that require future
          attention
       B. check on adequacy of past performance
       C. pinpoint responsibility for recurring daily tasks
       D. reduce the volume of material kept in general files

22. Which of the following BEST describes the process of   22.____
    reconciling a bank statement?
       A. Analyzing the nature of the expenditures made by the
          office during the preceding month
       B. Comparing the statement of the bank with the banking
          records maintained in the office
       C. Determining the liquidity position by reading the
          bank statement carefully
       D. Checking the service charges noted on the bank statement

23. From the viewpoint of preserving agency or institutional   23.____
    funds, which of the following is the LEAST acceptable
    method for making a payment?
    A check made out to
       A. cash   B. a company
       C. an individual   D. a partnership

24. In general, the CHIEF economy of using multicopy forms is   24.____
    in
       A. the paper on which the form is printed
       B. printing the form
       C. employee time
       D. carbon paper

25. Suppose your supervisor has asked you to develop a form   25.____
    to record certain information needed.
    The FIRST thing you should do is to
       A. determine the type of data that will be recorded
          repeatedly so that it can be preprinted

B. study the relationship of the form to the job to be accomplished so that the form can be planned
C. determine the information that will be recorded in the same place on each copy of the form so that it can be used as a check
D. find out who will be responsible for supplying the information so that space can be provided for their signatures

26. An administrative officer in charge of a small fund for buying office supplies has just written a check to Charles Laird, a supplier, and has sent the check by messenger to him. A half-hour later, the messenger telephones the administrative officer. He has lost the check.
Which of the following is the MOST important action for the administrative officer to take under these circumstances?
    A. Ask the messenger to return and write a report describing the loss of the check.
    B. Make a note on the performance record of the messenger who lost the check.
    C. Take the necessary steps to have payment stopped on the check.
    D. Refrain from doing anyting since the check may be found shortly.

26.____

27. A petty cash fund is set up PRIMARILY to
    A. take care of small investments that must be made from time to time
    B. take care of small expenses that arise from time to time
    C. provide a fund to be used as the office wants to use it with little need to maintain records
    D. take care of expenses that develop during emergencies, such as machine breakdowns and fires

27.____

28. Of the following, which is usually the MOST important guideline in writing business letters?
A letter should be
    A. neat
    B. written in a formalized style
    C. written in clear language intelligible to the reader
    D. written in the past tense

28.____

29. Suppose you are asked to edit a policy statement. You note that personal pronouns like *you*, *we*, and *I* are used freely.
Which of the following statements BEST applies to this use of personal pronouns?
It
    A. is proper usage because written business language should not be different from carefully spoken business language
    B. requires correction because it is ungrammatical
    C. is proper because it is clearer and has a warmer tone
    D. requires correction because policies should be expressed in an impersonal manner

29.____

30. Good business letters are coherent.
    To be coherent means to
    A. keep only one unifying idea in the message
    B. present the total message
    C. use simple, direct words for the message
    D. tie together the various ideas in the message

30.___

31. Proper division of a letter into paragraphs requires that
    the writer of business letters should, as much as possible,
    be sure that
    A. each paragraph is short
    B. each paragraph develops discussion of just one topic
    C. each paragraph repeats the theme of the total message
    D. there are at least two paragraphs for every message

31.___

32. An editor is given a letter with this initial paragraph:
    *We have received your letter, which we read with interest,
    and we are happy to respond to your question. In fact,
    we talked with several people in our office to get ideas
    to send to you.*
    Which of the following is it MOST reasonable for the
    editor to conclude?
    The paragraph is
    A. concise
    B. communicating something of value
    C. unnecessary
    D. coherent

32.___

33. As soon as you pick up the phone, a very angry caller
    begins immediately to complain about city agencies and
    red tape. He says that he has been shifted to two or
    three different offices. It turns out that he is seeking
    information which is not immediately available to you.
    You believe you know, however, where it can be found.
    Which of the following actions is the BEST one for you
    to take?
    A. To eliminate all confusion, suggest that the caller
       write the mayor stating explicitly what he wants.
    B. Apologize by telling the caller how busy city agencies
       now are, but also tell him directly that you do not
       have the information he needs.
    C. Ask for the caller's telephone number and assure him
       you will call back after you have checked further.
    D. Give the caller the name and telephone number of the
       person who might be able to help, but explain that
       you are not positive he will get results.

33.___

34. Suppose that one of your duties is to dictate responses
    to routine requests from the public for information. A
    letter writer asks for information which, as expressed in
    a one-sentence, explicit agency rule, cannot be given out
    to the public.
    Of the following ways of answering the letter, which is
    the MOST efficient?
    A. Quote verbatim that section of the agency rules which
       prohibits giving this information to the public.

34.___

    B. Without quoting the rule, explain why you cannot accede to the request and suggest alternative sources.
    C. Describe how carefully the request was considered before classifying it as subject to the rule forbidding the issuance of such information.
    D. Acknowledge receipt of the letter and advise that the requested information is not released to the public.

35. Suppose you assist in supervising a staff which has rather high morale, and your own supervisor asks you to poll the staff to find out who will be able to work overtime this particular evening to help complete emergency work.
    Which of the following approaches would be MOST likely to win their cooperation while maintaining their morale?
    A. Tell them that the better assignments will be given only to those who work overtime.
    B. Tell them that occasional overtime is a job requirement.
    C. Assure them they'll be doing you a personal favor.
    D. Let them know clearly why the overtime is needed.

35.____

36. Suppose that you have been asked to write and to prepare for reproduction new departmental vacation leave regulations.
    After you have written the new regulations, all of which fit on one page, which one of the following would be the BEST method of reproducing 1000 copies?
    A. An outside private printer, because you can best maintain confidentiality using this technique
    B. Xeroxing, because the copies will have the best possible appearance
    C. Typing carbon copies, because you will be certain that there are the fewest possible errors
    D. The multilith process, because it is quick and neat

36.____

37. Administration is the center, but not necessarily the source, of all ideas for procedural improvement.
    The MOST significant implication that this principle bears for the administrative officer is that
    A. before procedural improvements are introduced, they should be approved by a majority of the staff
    B. it is the unique function of the administrative officer to derive and introduce procedural improvements
    C. the administrative officer should derive ideas and suggestions for procedural improvement from all possible sources, introducing any that promise to be effective
    D. the administrative officer should view employee grievances as the chief source of procedural improvements

37.____

38. Your bureau is assigned an important task.   38.___
    Of the following, the function that you, as an administra-
    tive officer, can LEAST reasonably be expected to perform
    under these circumstances is
    A. division of the large job into individual tasks
    B. establishment of *production lines* within the bureau
    C. performance personally of a substantial share of all
       the work
    D. check-up to see that the work has been well done

39. Suppose that you have broken a complex job into its   39.___
    smaller components before making assignments to the
    employees under your jurisdiction.
    Of the following, the LEAST advisable procedure to follow
    from that point is to
    A. give each employee a picture of the importance of his
       work for the success of the total job
    B. establish a definite line of work flow and responsi-
       bility
    C. post a written memorandum of the best method for
       performing each job
    D. teach a number of alternative methods for doing each
       job

40. As an administrative officer, you are requested to draw   40.___
    up an organization chart of the whole department.
    Of the following, the MOST important characteristic of
    such a chart is that it will
    A. include all peculiarities and details of the organiza-
       tion which distinguish it from any other
    B. be a schematic representation of purely administra-
       tive functions within the department
    C. present a modification of the actual departmental
       organization in the light of principles of scientific
       management
    D. present an accurate picture of the lines of authority
       and responsibility

KEY (CORRECT ANSWERS)

1. A	11. B	21. A	31. B
2. C	12. D	22. B	32. C
3. C	13. C	23. A	33. C
4. D	14. B	24. C	34. A
5. D	15. D	25. B	35. D
6. C	16. A	26. C	36. B
7. D	17. C	27. B	37. C
8. B	18. A	28. C	38. C
9. C	19. C	29. D	39. D
10. C	20. A	30. D	40. D

TEST 2

DIRECTIONS: Each question or incomplete statement is followed by several suggested answers or completions. Select the one that BEST answers the question or completes the statement. *PRINT THE LETTER OF THE CORRECT ANSWER IN THE SPACE AT THE RIGHT.*

Questions 1-10.

DIRECTIONS: In each of Questions 1 through 10, a pair of related words written in capital letters is followed by four other pairs of words. For each question, select the pair of words which MOST closely expresses a relationship similar to that of the pair in capital letters.

SAMPLE QUESTION:

BOAT - DOCK
A. airplane - hangar   B. rain - snow
C. cloth - cotton   D. hunger - food

Choice A is the answer to this sample question since, of the choices given, the relationship between airplane and hangar is most similar to the relationship between boat and dock.

1. AUTOMOBILE - FACTORY   1.____
    A. tea - lemon   B. wheel - engine
    C. pot - flower   D. paper - mill

2. GIRDER - BRIDGE   2.____
    A. petal - flower   B. street- sidewalk
    C. meat - vegetable   D. sun - storm

3. RADIUS - CIRCLE   3.____
    A. brick - building   B. tie - tracks
    C. spoke - wheel   D. axle - tire

4. DISEASE - RESEARCH   4.____
    A. death - poverty   B. speech - audience
    C. problem - conference D. invalid - justice

5. CONCLUSION - INTRODUCTION   5.____
    A. commencement - beginning B. housing - motor
    C. caboose - engine   D. train - cabin

6. SOCIETY - LAW   6.____
    A. baseball - rules   B. jury - law
    C. cell - prisoner   D. sentence - jury

7. PLAN - ACCOMPLISHMENT   7.____
    A. deed - fact   B. method - success
    C. graph - chart   D. rules - manual

8. ORDER - GOVERNMENT   8.____
    A. chaos - administration   B. confusion - pandemonium
    C. rule - stability   D. despair - hope

9. TYRANNY - FREEDOM   9.____
    A. despot - mob   B. wealth - poverty
    C. nobility - commoners   D. dictatorship - democracy

10. TELEGRAM - LETTER   10.____
    A. hare - tortoise   B. lie - truth
    C. number - word   D. report - research

Questions 11-16.

DIRECTIONS: Answer Questions 11 through 16 SOLELY on the basis of
                 the information given in the passage below.

Inherent in all organized endeavors is the need to resolve the individual differences involved in conflict. Conflict may be either a positive or negative factor, since it may lead to creativity, innovation, and progress, on the one hand, or it may result, on the other hand, in a deterioration or even destruction of the organization. Thus, some forms of conflict are desirable, whereas others are undesirable and ethically wrong.

There are three management strategies which deal with inter-personal conflict. In the "divide-and-rule strategy", management attempts to maintain control by limiting the conflict to those directly involved and preventing their disagreement from spreading to the larger group. The "suppression-of-differences strategy" entails ignoring conflicts or pretending they are irrelevant. In the "working-through-differences strategy", management actively attempts to solve or resolve intergroup or interpersonal conflicts. Of the three strategies, only the last directly attacks and has the potential for eliminating the causes of conflict. An essential part of this strategy, however, is its employment by a committed and relatively mature management team.

11. According to the above passage, the *divide-and-rule*   11.____
    strategy for dealing with conflict is the attempt to
    A. involve other people in the conflict
    B. restrict the conflict to those participating in it
    C. divide the conflict into positive and negative factors
    D. divide the conflict into a number of smaller ones

12. The word *conflict* is used in relation to both positive and   12.____
    negative factors in this passage.
    Which one of the following words is MOST likely to describe
    the activity which the word *conflict*, in the sense of the
    passage, implies?
    A. Competition   B. Cooperation
    C. Confusion   D. Aggression

13. According to the above passage, which one of the following   13.___
    characteristics is shared by both the *suppression-of-
    differences strategy* and the *divide-and-rule strategy*?
    A. Pretending that conflicts are irrelevant
    B. Preventing conflicts from spreading to the group
       situation
    C. Failure to directly attack the causes of conflict
    D. Actively attempting to resolve interpersonal conflict

14. According to the above passage, the successful resolution   14.___
    of interpersonal conflict requires
    A. allowing the group to mediate conflicts between two
       individuals
    B. division of the conflict into positive and negative
       factors
    C. involvement of a committed, mature management team
    D. ignoring minor conflicts until they threaten the
       organization

15. Which can be MOST reasonably inferred from the above   15.___
    passage?
    A conflict between two individuals is LEAST likely to
    continue when management uses
    A. the *working-through-differences strategy*
    B. the *suppression-of-differences strategy*
    C. the *divide-and-rule strategy*
    D. a combination of all three strategies

16. According to the above passage, a desirable result of   16.___
    conflict in an organization is when conflict
    A. exposes production problems in the organization
    B. can be easily ignored by management
    C. results in advancement of more efficient managers
    D. leads to development of new methods

Questions 17-23.

DIRECTIONS: Answer Questions 17 through 23 SOLELY on the basis of
               the information given in the passage below.

*Modern management places great emphasis on the concept of
communication. The communication process consists of the steps
through which an idea or concept passes from its inception by one
person, the sender, until it is acted upon by another person, the
receiver. Through an understanding of these steps and some of the
possible barriers that may occur, more effective communication may
be achieved. The first step in the communication process is ideation
by the sender. This is the formation of the intended content of the
message he wants to transmit. In the next step, encoding, the sender
organizes his ideas into a series of symbols designed to communicate
his message to his intended receiver. He selects suitable words or
phrases that can be understood by the receiver, and he also selects
the appropriate media to be used -- for example, memorandum, conference, etc. The third step is transmission of the encoded message
through selected channels in the organizational structure. In the
fourth step, the receiver enters the process by tuning in to receive*

*the message. If the receiver does not function, however, the
message is lost. For example, if the message is oral, the receiver
must be a good listener. The fifth step is decoding of the message
by the receiver, as for example, by changing words into ideas. At
this step, the decoded message may not be the same idea that the
sender originally encoded because the sender and receiver have
different perceptions regarding the meaning of certain words.
Finally, the receiver acts or responds. He may file the information,
ask for more information, or take other action. There can be no
assurance, however, that communication has taken place unless there
is some type of feedback to the sender in the form of an acknowledge-
ment that the message was received.*

17. According to the above passage, *ideation* is the process   17.___
    by which the
    A. sender develops the intended content of the message
    B. sender organizes his ideas into a series of symbols
    C. receiver tunes in to receive the message
    D. receiver decodes the message

18. In the last sentence of the passage, the word *feedback*   18.___
    refers to the process by which the sender is assured that
    the
    A. receiver filed the information
    B. receiver's perception is the same as his own
    C. message was received
    D. message was properly interpreted

19. Which one of the following BEST shows the order of the   19.___
    steps in the communication process as described in the
    passage?
        A. 1 - ideation   2 - encoding
           3 - decoding   4 - transmission
           5 - receiving   6 - action
           7 - feedback to the sender

        B. 1 - ideation   2 - encoding
           3 - transmission   4 - decoding
           5 - receiving   6 - action
           7 - feedback to the sender

        C. 1 - ideation   2 - decoding
           3 - transmission   4 - receiving
           5 - encoding   6 - action
           7 - feedback to the sender

        D. 1 - ideation   2 - encoding
           3 - transmission   4 - receiving
           5 - decoding   6 - action
           7 - feedback to the sender

20. Which one of the following BEST expresses the main theme   20.___
    of the passage?
        A. Different individuals have the same perceptions
           regarding the meaning of words.

B. An understanding of the steps in the communication process may achieve better communication.
C. Receivers play a passive role in the communication process.
D. Senders should not communicate with receivers who transmit feedback.

21. The above passage implies that a receiver does NOT function properly when he   21.___
    A. transmits feedback   B. files the information
    C. is a poor listener   D. asks for more information

22. Which of the following, according to the above passage,   22.___
is included in the SECOND step of the communication process?
    A. Selecting the appropriate media to be used in transmission
    B. Formulation of the intended content of the message
    C. Using appropriate media to respond to the receiver's feedback
    D. Transmitting the message through selected channels in the organization

23. The above passage implies that the *decoding process* is   23.___
MOST NEARLY the reverse of the ____ process.
    A. transmission   B. receiving
    C. feedback   D. encoding

Questions 24-27.

DIRECTIONS: Answer Questions 24 through 27 SOLELY on the basis of the information given in the paragraph below.

A personnel researcher has at his disposal various approaches for obtaining information, analyzing it, and arriving at conclusions that have value in predicting and affecting the behavior of people at work. The type of method to be used depends on such factors as the nature of the research problem, the available data, and the attitudes of those people being studied to the various kinds of approaches. While the experimental approach, with its use of control groups, is the most refined type of study, there are others that are often found useful in personnel research. Surveys, in which the researcher obtains facts on a problem from a variety of sources, are employed in research on wages, fringe benefits, and labor relations. Historical studies are used to trace the development of problems in order to understand them better and to isolate possible causative factors. Case studies are generally developed to explore all the details of a particular problem that is representative of other similar problems. A researcher chooses the most appropriate form of study for the problem he is investigating. He should recognize, however, that the experimental method, commonly referred to as the scientific method, if used validly and reliably, gives the most conclusive results.

24. The above statement discusses several approaches used to   24.___
    obtain information on particular problems.
    Which of the following may be MOST reasonably concluded
    from the paragraph?
    A(n)
      A. historical study cannot determine causative factors
      B. survey is often used in research on fringe benefits
      C. case study is usually used to explore a problem that
         is unique and unrelated to other problems
      D. experimental study is used when the scientific
         approach to a problem fails

25. According to the above paragraph, all of the following   25.___
    are factors that may determine the type of approach a
    researcher uses EXCEPT
      A. the attitudes of people toward being used in control
         groups
      B. the number of available sources
      C. his desire to isolate possible causative factors
      D. the degree of accuracy he requires

26. The words *scientific method*, used in the last sentence   26.___
    of the paragraph, refer to a type of study which, according
    to the paragraph,
      A. uses a variety of sources
      B. traces the development of problems
      C. uses control groups
      D. analyzes the details of a representative problem

27. Which of the following can be MOST reasonably concluded   27.___
    from the above paragraph?
    In obtaining and analyzing information on a particular
    problem, a researcher employs the method which is the
      A. most accurate   B. most suitable
      C. least expensive   D. least time-consuming

Questions 28-31.

DIRECTIONS: The graph below indicates at 5-year intervals the
number of citations issued for various offenses from
the year 1950 to the year 1970. Answer Questions 28
through 31 according to the information given in this
graph.

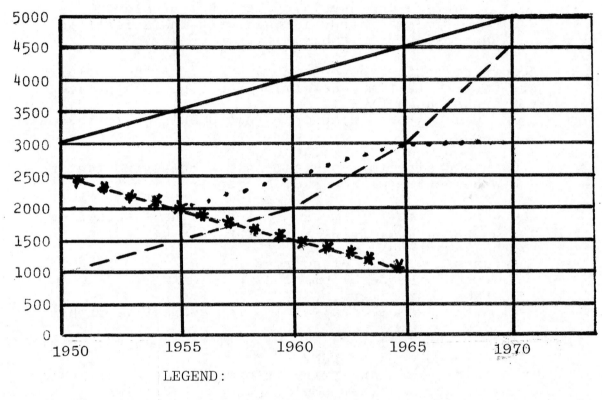

LEGEND:

——————— Parking Violations

— — — Drug Use

· · · · Dangerous Weapons

✳—✳—✳—✳ Improper Dress

28. Over the 20-year period, which offense shows an AVERAGE   28.___
    rate of increase of more than 150 citations per year?
       A. Parking Violations   B. Dangerous Weapons
       C. Drug Use   D. None of the above

29. Over the 20-year period, which offense shows a CONSTANT   29.___
    rate of increase or decrease?
       A. Parking Violations   B. Drug Use
       C. Dangerous Weapons   D. Improper Dress

30. Which offense shows a TOTAL INCREASE OR DECREASE of 50%   30.___
    for the full 20-year period?
       A. Parking Violations   B. Drug Use
       C. Dangerous Weapons   D. Improper Dress

31. The percentage increase in total citations issued from   31.___
    1955 to 1960 is MOST NEARLY
    A. 7%   B. 11%   C. 21%   D. 41%

Questions 32-35.

DIRECTIONS: The chart below shows the annual average number of
               administrative actions completed for the four divisions
               of a bureau. Assume that the figures remain stable
               from year to year.

               Answer Questions 32 through 35 SOLELY on the basis of
               information given in the chart.

Administrative Actions	DIVISIONS				Totals
	W	X	Y	Z	
Telephone Inquiries Answered	8,000	6,800	7,500	4,800	27,100
Interviews Conducted	500	630	550	500	2,180
Applications Processed	15,000	18,000	14,500	9,500	57,000
Letters Typed	2,500	4,400	4,350	3,250	14,500
Reports Completed	200	250	100	50	600
Totals	26,200	30,080	27,000	18,100	101,380

32. In which division is the number of Applications Processed   32.___
    the GREATEST percentage of the total Administrative
    Actions for that division?
    A. W   B. X   C. Y   D. Z

33. The bureau chief is considering a plan that would consoli-   33.___
    date the typing of letters in a separate unit. This unit
    would be responsible for the typing of letters for all
    divisions in which the number of letters typed exceeds
    15% of the total number of Administrative Actions.
    Under this plan, which of the following divisions would
    CONTINUE to type its own letters?
    A. W and X   B. W, X, and Y
    C. X and Y   D. X and Z

34. The setting up of a central information service that
    would be capable of answering 25% of the whole bureau's
    telephone inquiries is under consideration. Under such
    a plan, the divisions would gain for other activities that
    time previously spent on telephone inquiries.
    Approximately how much total time would such a service
    gain for all four divisions if it requires 5 minutes to
    answer the average telephone inquiry? _____ hours.
    A. 500   B. 515   C. 565   D. 585

34. ___

35. Assume that the rate of production shown in the table can
    be projected as accurate for the coming year and that
    monthly output is constant for each type of administrative
    action within a division. Division Y is scheduled to work
    exclusively on a 4-month long special project during that
    year. During the period of the project, Division Y's
    regular workload will be divided evenly among the remaining
    divisions.
    Using the figures in the table, what would be MOST NEARLY
    the percentage increase in the total Administrative Actions
    completed by Division Z for the year?
    A. 8%   B. 16%   C. 25%   D. 50%

35. ___

36. You have conducted a traffic survey at 10 two-lane
    bridges and find the traffic between 4:30 and 5:30 P.M.
    averages 665 cars per bridge that hour. You can't find
    the tabulation sheet for Bridge #7, but you know that
    6066 cars were counted at the other 9 bridges.
    Determine from this how many must have been counted at
    Bridge #7.
    A. 584   B. 674   C. 665   D. 607

36. ___

37. You pay temporary help $5.60 per hour and regular
    employees $6.00 per hour. Your workload is temporarily
    heavy, so you need 20 hours of extra regular employees'
    time to catch up. If you do this on overtime, you must
    pay time-and-a-half. If you use temporary help, it takes
    25% more time to do the job.
    What is the difference in cost between the two alternatives?
    A. $10 more for temporary   B. $20 more for temporary
    C. $40 more for regular   D. $68 more for regular

37. ___

38. An experienced clerk can process the mailing of annual
    forms in 9 days. A new clerk takes 14 days to process
    them.
    If they work together, how many days MOST NEARLY will it
    take to do the processing?
    A. 4½   B. 5½   C. 6½   D. 7

38. ___

39. A certain administrative aide is usually able to success-
    fully handle 27% of all telephone inquiries without
    assistance. In a particular month, he receives 1200
    inquiries and handles 340 of them successfully on his own.
    How many more inquiries has he handled successfully in
    that month than would have been expected of him based on
    his usual rate?
    A. 10   B. 16   C. 24   D. 44

39. ___

40. Suppose that on a scaled drawing of an office building   40.___
    floor, ½ inch represents three feet of actual floor
    dimensions.
    A floor which is, in fact, 75 feet wide and 132 feet long
    has which of the following dimensions on this scaled
    drawing? ____ inches wide and ____ inches long.
    A. 9.5; 20.5   B. 12.5; 22
    C. 17; 32   D. 25; 44

41. In a division of clerks and stenographers, 15 people are   41.___
    currently employed, 20% of whom are stenographers.
    If management plans are to maintain the current number of
    stenographers, but to increase the clerical staff to the
    point where 12% of the total staff are stenographers, what
    is the MAXIMUM number of additional clerks that should
    be hired to meet these plans?
    A. 3   B. 8   C. 10   D. 12

42. Suppose that a certain agency had a 1985 budget of   42.___
    $1,100,500. The 1986 budget was 7% higher than that of
    1985, and the 1987 budget was 8% higher than that of 1986.
    Of the following, which one is MOST NEARLY that agency's
    budget for 1987?
    A. $1,117,624   B. $1,261,737
    C. $1,265,575   D. $1,271,738

Questions 43-50.

DIRECTIONS: Your office keeps a file card record of the work
               assignments for all the employees in a certain bureau.
               On each card is the employee's name, a work assignment
               code number, and the date of this assignment. In this
               filing system, the employee's name is filed alpha-
               betically, the work assignment code is filed numerically,
               and the date of the assignment is filed chronologically
               (earliest date first).

               Each of Questions 43 through 50 represents five cards
               to be filed, numbered (1) through (5) shown in Column I.
               Each card is made up of the employee's name, a work
               assignment code number shown in parentheses, and the
               date of this assignment. The cards are to be filed
               according to the following rules:

    First: File in alphabetical order;
    Second: When two or more cards have the same employee's name,
            file according to the work assignment number, beginning
            with the lowest number.
    Third: When two or more cards have the same employee's name
           and same assignment number, file according to the
           assignment date beginning with earliest date.

               Column II shows the cards arranged in four different
               orders. Pick the answer (A, B, C, or D) in Column II
               which shows the cards arranged correctly according to
               the above filing rules.

SAMPLE QUESTION:

Column I				Column II
(1) Cluney	(486503)	6/17/72		A. 2, 3, 4, 1, 5
(2) Roster	(246611)	5/10/71		B. 2, 5, 1, 3, 4
(3) Altool	(711433)	10/15/72		C. 3, 2, 1, 4, 5
(4) Cluney	(527610)	12/18/71		D. 3, 5, 1, 4, 2
(5) Cluney	(486500)	4/8/72		

The correct way to file the cards is:
(3) Altool (711433) 10/15/72
(5) Cluney (486500)   4/8/72
(1) Cluney (486503) 6/17/72
(4) Cluney (527610) 12/18/71
(2) Roster (246611)   5/10/71

The correct filing order is shown by the numbers in front of each
name (3, 5, 1, 4, 2). The answer to the sample question is the
letter in Column II in front of the numbers 3, 5, 1, 4, 2. This
answer is D.

Column I				Column II	
43. (1) Prichard	(013469)	4/6/71		A. 5, 4, 3, 2, 1	43.___
(2) Parks	(678941)	2/7/71		B. 1, 2, 5, 3, 4	
(3) Williams	(551467)	3/6/70		C. 2, 1, 5, 3, 4	
(4) Wilson	(551466)	8/9/67		D. 1, 5, 4, 3, 2	
(5) Stanhope	(300014)	8/9/67			
44. (1) Ridgeway	(623809)	8/11/71		A. 5, 1, 3, 4, 2	44.___
(2) Travers	(305439)	4/5/67		B. 5, 1, 3, 2, 4	
(3) Tayler	(818134)	7/5/68		C. 1, 5, 3, 2, 4	
(4) Travers	(305349)	5/6/70		D. 1, 5, 4, 2, 3	
(5) Ridgeway	(623089)	10/9/71			
45. (1) Jaffe	(384737)	2/19/71		A. 3, 5, 2, 4, 1	45.___
(2) Inez	(859176)	8/8/72		B. 3, 5, 2, 1, 4	
(3) Ingrahm	(946460)	8/6/69		C. 2, 3, 5, 1, 4	
(4) Karp	(256146)	5/5/70		D. 2, 3, 5, 4, 1	
(5) Ingrahm	(946460)	6/4/70			
46. (1) Marrano	(369421)	7/24/69		A. 1, 5, 3, 4, 2	46.___
(2) Marks	(652910)	2/23/71		B. 3, 5, 4, 2, 1	
(3) Netto	(556772)	3/10/72		C. 2, 4, 1, 5, 3	
(4) Marks	(652901)	2/17/72		D. 4, 2, 1, 5, 3	
(5) Netto	(556772)	6/17/70			
47. (1) Abernathy	(712467)	6/23/70		A. 5, 3, 1, 2, 4	47.___
(2) Acevedo	(680262)	6/23/68		B. 5, 4, 2, 3, 1	
(3) Aaron	(967647)	1/17/69		C. 1, 3, 5, 2, 4	
(4) Acevedo	(680622)	5/14/67		D. 2, 4, 1, 5, 3	
(5) Aaron	(967647)	4/1/65			

48. (1) Simon   (645219) 8/19/70   A. 4, 1, 2, 5, 3   48.____
    (2) Simon   (645219) 9/2/68   B. 4, 5, 2, 1, 3
    (3) Simons   (645218) 7/7/70   C. 3, 5, 2, 1, 4
    (4) Simms   (646439) 10/12/71   D. 5, 1, 2, 3, 4
    (5) Simon   (645219) 10/16/67

49. (1) Rappaport (312230) 6/11/71   A. 4, 3, 1, 2, 5   49.____
    (2) Rascio   (777510) 2/9/70   B. 4, 3, 1, 5, 2
    (3) Rappaport (312230) 7/3/67   C. 3, 4, 1, 5, 2
    (4) Rapaport (312330) 9/6/70   D. 5, 2, 4, 3, 1
    (5) Rascio   (777501) 7/7/70

50. (1) Johnson (843250) 6/8/67   A. 1, 3, 2, 4, 5   50.____
    (2) Johnson (843205) 4/3/70   B. 1, 3, 2, 5, 4
    (3) Johnson (843205) 8/6/67   C. 3, 2, 1, 4, 5
    (4) Johnson (843602) 3/8/71   D. 3, 2, 1, 5, 4
    (5) Johnson (843602) 8/3/70

KEY (CORRECT ANSWERS)

1. D	11. B	21. C	31. B	41. C
2. A	12. A	22. A	32. B	42. D
3. C	13. C	23. D	33. A	43. C
4. C	14. C	24. B	34. C	44. A
5. C	15. A	25. D	35. B	45. C
6. A	16. D	26. C	36. A	46. D
7. B	17. A	27. B	37. C	47. A
8. C	18. C	28. C	38. B	48. B
9. D	19. D	29. A	39. B	49. B
10. A	20. B	30. C	40. B	50. D

EXAMINATION SECTION
TEST 1

DIRECTIONS: Each question or incomplete statement is followed by several suggested answers or completions. Select the one that BEST answers the question or completes the statement. *PRINT THE LETTER OF THE CORRECT ANSWER IN THE SPACE AT THE RIGHT.*

Questions 1-6.

DIRECTIONS: Questions 1 through 6 each consist of four sentences. Choose the one sentence in each set of four that would be BEST for a formal letter or report. Consider grammar and appropriate usage.

1. A. These statements can be depended on, for their truth   1.___
    has been guaranteed by reliable city employees.
    B. Reliable city employees guarantee the facts with regards
    to the truth of these statements.
    C. Most all these statements have been supported by city
    employees who are reliable and can be depended upon.
    D. The city employees which have guaranteed these state-
    ments are reliable.

2. A. I believe the letter was addressed to either my   2.___
    associate or I.
    B. If properly addressed, the letter will reach my
    associate and I.
    C. My associate's name, as well as mine, was on the
    letter.
    D. The letter had been addressed to myself and my
    associate.

3. A. The secretary would have corrected the errors if she   3.___
    knew that the supervisor would see the report.
    B. The supervisor reprimanded the secretary, whom she
    believed had made careless errors.
    C. Many errors were found in the report which she typed
    and could not disregard them.
    D. The errors in the typed report were so numerous that
    they could hardly be overlooked.

4. A. His consultant was as pleased as he with the success   4.___
    of the project.
    B. The success of the project pleased both his consultant
    and he.
    C. He and also his consultant was pleased with the success
    of the project.
    D. Both his consultant and he was pleased with the success
    of the project.

5. A. Since the letter did not contain the needed information, 5.___
   it was not real useful to him.
   B. Being that the letter lacked the needed information,
   he could not use it.
   C. Since the letter lacked the needed information, it
   was of no use to him.
   D. This letter was useless to him because there was no
   needed information in it.

6. A. Scarcely had the real estate tax increase been declared 6.___
   than the notices were sent out.
   B. They had no sooner declared the real estate tax
   increases when they sent the notices to the owners.
   C. The city had hardly declared the real estate tax
   increase till the notices were prepared for mailing.
   D. No sooner had the real estate tax increase been
   declared than the notices were sent out.

Questions 7-14.

DIRECTIONS: Answer Questions 7 through 14 on the basis of the
following passage.

Important figures in education and in public affairs have
recommended development of a private organization sponsored in part
by various private foundations which would offer installment payment
plans to full-time matriculated students in accredited colleges and
universities in the United States and Canada. Contracts would be
drawn to cover either tuition and fees, or tuition, fees, room and
board in college facilities, from one year up to and including six
years. A special charge, which would vary with the length of the
contract, would be added to the gross repayable amount. This would
be in addition to interest at a rate which would vary with the
income of the parents. There would be a 3% annual interest charge
for families with total income, before income taxes of $10,000 or
less. The rate would increase by 1/10 of 1% for every $200 of
additional net income in excess of $10,000 up to a maximum of 10%
interest. Contracts would carry an insurance provision on the life
of the parent or guardian who signs the contract; all contracts
must have the signature of a parent or guardian. Payment would be
scheduled in equal monthly installments.

7. Which of the following students would be eligible for 7.___
   the payment plan described in the above passage?
   A
   A. matriculated student taking 6 semester hours toward
   a graduate degree at CCNY
   B. matriculated student taking 17 semester hours toward
   an undergraduate degree at Brooklyn College
   C. CCNY graduate matriculated at the University of
   Mexico, taking 18 semester hours toward a graduate
   degree
   D. student taking 18 semester hours in a special pre-
   matriculation program at Hunter College

8. According to the above passage, the organization described   8.___
   would be sponsored in part by
     A. private foundations
     B. colleges and universities
     C. persons in the field of education
     D. persons in public life

9. Which of the following expenses could NOT be covered by   9.___
   a contract with the organization described in the above
   passage?
     A. Tuition amounting to $4,000 per year
     B. Registration and laboratory fees
     C. Meals at restaurants near the college
     D. Rent for an apartment in a college dormitory

10. The total amount to be paid would include ONLY the   10.___
     A. principal
     B. principal and interest
     C. principal, interest, and special charge
     D. principal, interest, special charge, and fee

11. The contract would carry insurance on the   11.___
     A. life of the student
     B. life of the student's parents
     C. income of the parents of the student
     D. life of the parent who signed the contract

12. The interest rate for an annual loan of $5,000 from the   12.___
    organization described in the passage for a student whose
    family's net income was $11,000 should be
     A. 3%   B. 3.5%   C. 4%   D. 4.5%

13. The interest rate for an annual loan of $7,000 from the   13.___
    organization described in the passage for a student whose
    family's net income was $20,000 should be
     A. 5%   B. 8%   C. 9%   D. 10%

14. John Lee has submitted an application for the installment   14.___
    payment plan described in the passage. John's mother and
    father have a store which grossed $100,000 last year, but
    the income which the family received from the store was
    $18,000 before taxes. They also had $1,000 income from
    stock dividends. They paid $2,000 in income taxes.
    The amount of income upon which the interest should be
    based is
     A. $17,000   B. $18,000   C. $19,000   D. $21,000

15. One of the MOST important techniques for conducting   15.___
    good interviews is
     A. asking the applicant questions in rapid succession,
        thereby keeping the conversation properly focused
     B. listening carefully to all that the applicant has to
        say, making mental notes of possible areas for follow-
        up

C. indicating to the applicant the criteria and standards on which you will base your judgment
D. making sure that you are interrupted above five
   minutes before you wish to end so that you can keep
   on schedule

16. You are planning to conduct preliminary interviews of
    applicants for an important position in your department.
    Which of the following planning considerations is LEAST
    likely to contribute to successful interviews?
    A. Make provisions to conduct interviews in privacy
    B. Schedule your appointments so that interviews will
       be short
    C. Prepare a list of your objectives
    D. Learn as much as you can about the applicant before
       the interview.

16.___

17. In interviewing job applicants, which of the following
    usually does NOT have to be done before the end of the
    interview?
    A. Making a decision to hire an applicant
    B. Securing information from applicants
    C. Giving information to applicants
    D. Establishing a friendly relationship with applicants

17.___

18. In the process of interviewing applicants for a position
    on your staff, the one of the following which would be
    BEST is to
    A. make sure all applicants are introduced to the other
       members of your staff prior to the formal interview
    B. make sure the applicant does not ask questions about
       the job or the department
    C. avoid having the applicant talk with the staff under
       any circumstances
    D. introduce applicants to some of the staff at the
       conclusion of a successful interview

18.___

19. While interviewing a job applicant, you ask why the
    applicant left his last job. The applicant does not
    answer immediately.
    Of the following, the BEST action to take at that point
    is to
    A. wait until he answers
    B. ask another question
    C. repeat the question in a loud voice
    D. ask him why he does not answer

19.___

20. Which of the following actions would be LEAST desirable
    for you to take when you have to conduct an interview?
    A. Set a relaxed and friendly atmosphere
    B. Plan your interview ahead of time
    C. Allow the person interviewed to structure the inter-
       view as he wishes
    D. Include some stock or standard question which you
       ask everyone

20.___

21. You know that a student applying for a job in your office   21.___
    has done well in college except for two courses in
    science. However, when you ask him about his grades, his
    reply is vague and general.
    It would be BEST for you to
       A. lead the applicant to admitting doing poorly in
          science to be sure that the facts are correct
       B. judge the applicant's tact and skill in handling
          what may be for him a personally sensitive question
       C. immediately confront the applicant with the facts and
          ask for an explanation
       D. ignore the applicant's response since you have the
          transcript

22. A college student has applied for a position with your   22.___
    department. Prior to conducting an interview of the
    job applicant, it would be LEAST helpful for you to have
       A. a personal resume   B. a job description
       C. references   D. hiring requirements

23. Job applicants tend to be nervous during interviews.   23.___
    Which of the following techniques is MOST likely to put
    such an applicant at ease?
       A. Try to establish rapport by asking general questions
          which are easily answered by the applicant
       B. Ask the applicant to describe his career objectives
          immediately, thus minimizing the anxiety caused by
          waiting
       C. Start the interview with another member of the staff
          present so that the applicant does not feel alone
       D. Proceed as rapidly as possible, since the emotional
          state of the applicant is none of your concern

24. Of the following abilities, the one which is LEAST impor-   24.___
    tant in conducting an interview is the ability to
       A. ask the interviewee pertinent questions
       B. evaluate the interviewee on the basis of appearance
       C. evaluate the responses of the interviewee
       D. gain the cooperation of the interviewee

25. One of the techniques of management often used by super-   25.___
    visors is performance appraisal.
    Which of the following is NOT one of the objectives of
    performance appraisal?
       A. Improve staff performance
       B. Determine individual training needs
       C. Improve organizational structure
       D. Set standards and performance criteria for employees

KEY (CORRECT ANSWERS)

1. A	11. D
2. C	12. B
3. D	13. B
4. A	14. C
5. C	15. B
6. D	16. B
7. B	17. A
8. A	18. D
9. C	19. A
10. C	20. C

21. B
22. C
23. A
24. B
25. C

———

TEST 2

1. Examine the following sentence, and then choose the BEST   1.___
   statement about it from the choices below.
   Clerks are expected to receive visitors, to answer tele-
   phones, and miscellaneous clerical work must be done.
   A. This sentence is an example of effective writing.
   B. This is a *run-on* sentence.
   C. The three ideas in this sentence are not parallel,
      and therefore they should be divided into separate
      sentences.
   D. The three ideas in this sentence are parallel, but
      they are not expressed in parallel form.

2. Examine the following sentence, and then choose from   2.___
   below the word which should be inserted in the blank
   space.
   Mr. Luce is a top-notch interviewer, _____ he is very
   reliable.
   A. but   B. and   C. however   D. for

3. Examine the following sentence, and then choose from   3.___
   below the words which should be inserted in the blank
   spaces.
   The committee _____ sent in _____ report.
   A. has; it's   B. has; their
   C. have; its   D. has; its

4. Examine the following sentence, and then choose from   4.___
   below the words which should be inserted in the blank
   spaces.
   An organization usually contains more than just a few
   people; usually the membership is _____ enough so that
   close personal relationships among _____ impossible.
   A. large; are   B. large; found
   C. small; becomes   D. small; is

5. Of the following, the BEST reference book to use to find   5.___
   a synonym for a common word is a(n)
   A. thesaurus   B. dictionary
   C. encyclopedia   D. catalog

Questions 6-10.

DIRECTIONS: Questions 6 through 10 concern college students who
have just completed their junior year for whom you
must calculate grade averages for the year. These
averages are to be based on the following table showing the number of credit hours for each student during
the year at each of the grade levels: A, B, C, D, and
F. How these letter grades may be translated into
numerical grades is indicated in the first column of
the table.

Grade Value	Credit Hours – Junior Year					
	King	Lewis	Martin	Nonkin	Ottly	Perry
A = 95	12	6	15	3	9	–
B = 85	9	15	6	12	9	3
C = 75	6	9	9	12	3	27
D = 65	3	–	3	3	6	–
F = 0	–	–	–	3	–	–

Calculating a grade average for an individual student is a 4-
step process:
I. Multiply each grade value by the number of credit hours
for which the student received that grade
II. Add these multiplication products for each student
III. Add the student's total credit hours
IV. Divide the multiplication product total by the total
number of credit hours
V. Round the result, if there is a decimal place, to the
nearest whole number. A number ending in .5 would be
rounded to the next higher number

Example

Using student King's grades as an example, his grade average
can be calculated by going through the following four steps:

I. $95 \times 12 = 1140$
$85 \times 9 = 765$
$75 \times 6 = 450$
$65 \times 3 = 195$
$0 \times 0 = 0$

II. Total = 2550

III. 12
9
6
3
0
30 TOTAL credit hours

IV. Divide 2550 by 30: $\frac{2550}{30} = 85$

King's grade average is 85.

Answer Questions 6 through 10 on the basis of the information
given above.

6. The grade average of Lewis is
   A. 83   B. 84   C. 85   D. 86   6.___

7. The grade average of Martin is
   A. 83   B. 84   C. 85   D. 86   7.___

8. The grade average of Nonkin is
   A. 72   B. 73   C. 79   D. 80   8.___

9. Student Ottly must attain a grade average of 85 in each   9.___
   of his years in college to be accepted into graduate
   school.
   If, in summer school during his junior year, he takes
   two 3-credit courses and receives a grade of 85 in one
   and 95 in the other, his grade average for his junior
   year will then be MOST NEARLY
   A. 82   B. 83   C. 84   D. 85

10. If Perry takes an additional 3-credit course during the   10.___
    year and receives a grade of 95, his grade average will
    be increased to approximately
    A. 74   B. 76   C. 78   D. 80

11. You are in charge of verifying employees' qualifications.   11.___
    This involves telephoning previous employers and schools.
    One of the applications which you are reviewing contains
    information which you are almost certain is correct on
    the basis of what the employee has told you.
    The BEST thing to do is to
       A. check the information again with the employee
       B. perform the required verification procedures
       C. accept the information as valid
       D. ask a superior to verify the information

12. The practice of immediately identifying oneself and one's   12.___
    place of employment when contacting persons on the tele-
    phone is
       A. *good*, because the receiver of the call can quickly
          identify the caller and establish a frame of
          reference
       B. *good*, because it helps to set the caller at ease
          with the other party
       C. *poor*, because it is not necessary to divulge that
          information when making general calls
       D. *poor*, because it takes longer to arrive at the topic
          to be discussed

13. A supervisor, Miss Smith, meets with a group of sub-   13.___
    ordinates and tells them how they should perform certain
    tasks. The meeting is highly successful. She then
    attends a meeting to discuss common problems with a group
    of fellow supervisors with duties similar to her own.
    When she tells them how their subordinates should perform
    the same tasks, some of the other supervisors become angry.

Of the following, the MOST likely reason for this anger is that
  A. tension is to be expected in situations in which supervisors deal with each other
  B. the other supervisors are jealous of Miss Smith's knowledge
  C. Miss Smith should not tell other supervisors what methods she uses
  D. Miss Smith does not correctly perceive her role in relation to other supervisors

14. There is considerable rivalry among employees in a certain department over location of desks. It is the practice of the supervisor to assign desks without any predetermined plan. The supervisor is reconsidering his procedure.
    In assigning desks, PRIMARY consideration should ordinarily be given to
      A. past practices
      B. flow of work
      C. employee seniority
      D. social relations among employees

15. Assume that, when you tell some of the typists under your supervision that the letters they prepare have too many errors, they contend that the letters are readable and that they obtain more satisfaction from their jobs if they do not have to be as concerned about errors.
    These typists are
      A. *correct*, because the ultimate objective should be job satisfaction
      B. *incorrect*, because every job should be performed perfectly
      C. *correct*, because they do not compose the letters themselves
      D. *incorrect*, because their satisfaction is not the only consideration

16. Which of the following possible conditions is LEAST likely to represent a hindrance to effective communication?
      A. The importance of a situation may not be apparent.
      B. Words may mean different things to different people.
      C. The recipient of a communication may respond to it, sometimes unfavorably.
      D. Communications may affect the self-interest of those communicating.

17. You are revising the way in which your unit handles records.
    One of the BEST ways to make sure that the change will be implemented with a minimum of difficulty is to

14.___

15.___

16.___

17.___

A. allow everyone on the staff who is affected by the change to have an opportunity to contribute their ideas to the new procedures
B. advise only the key members of your staff in advance so that they can help you enforce the new method when it is implemented
C. give the assignment of implementation to the newest member of the unit
D. issue a memorandum announcing the change and stating that complaints will not be tolerated

18. One of your assistants is quite obviously having personal problems that are affecting his work performance.
As a supervisor, it would be MOST appropriate for you to
A. avoid any inquiry into the nature of the situation since this is not one of your responsibilities
B. avoid any discussion of personal problems on the basis that there is nothing you could do about them anyhow
C. help the employee obtain appropriate help with these problems
D. advise the employee that personal problems cannot be considered when evaluating work performance

18.___

19. The key to improving communication with your staff and other departments is the development of an awareness of the importance of communication.
Which of the following is NOT a good suggestion for developing this awareness?
A. Be willing to look at your own attitude toward how you communicate
B. Be sensitive and receptive to reactions to what you tell people
C. Make sure all communication is in writing
D. When giving your subordinates directions, try to put yourself in their place and see if your instructions still make sense

19.___

20. One of the assistants on your staff has neglected to complete an important assignment on schedule. You feel that a reprimand is necessary.
When speaking to the employee, it would usually be LEAST desirable to
A. display your anger to show the employee how strongly you feel about the problem
B. ask several questions about the reasons for failure to complete the assignment
C. take the employee aside so that nobody else is present when you discuss the matter
D. give the employee as much time as he needs to explain exactly what happened

20.___

KEY (CORRECT ANSWERS)

1.	D	11.	B
2.	B	12.	A
3.	D	13.	D
4.	A	14.	B
5.	A	15.	D
6.	B	16.	C
7.	C	17.	A
8.	B	18.	C
9.	C	19.	C
10.	C	20.	A

EXAMINATION SECTION
TEST 1

DIRECTIONS: Each question or incomplete statement is followed by several suggested answers or completions. Select the one that BEST answers the question or completes the statement. *PRINT THE LETTER OF THE CORRECT ANSWER IN THE SPACE AT THE RIGHT.*

1. Assume that you are a supervisor of a unit which is about to start work on an urgent job. One of your subordinates starts to talk to you about the urgent job but seems not to be saying what is really on his mind.
   What is the BEST thing for you to say under these circumstances?
   A. *I'm not sure I understand. Can you explain that?*
   B. *Please come to the point. We haven't got all day.*
   C. *What is it? Can't you see I'm busy?*
   D. *Haven't you got work to do? What do you want?*

1.___

2. Assume that you have recently been assigned a new subordinate. You have explained to this subordinate how to fill out certain forms which will constitute the major portion of her job. After the first day, you find that she has filled out the forms correctly but has not completed as many as most other workers normally complete in a day.
   Of the following, the MOST appropriate action for you to take is to
   A. tell the subordinate how many forms she is expected to complete
   B. instruct the subordinate in the correct method of filling out the forms
   C. monitor the subordinate's production to see if she improves
   D. reassign the job of filling out the forms to a more experienced worker in the unit

2.___

3. One of the problems commonly met by the supervisor is the *touchy* employee who imagines slights when none are intended.
   Of the following, the BEST way to deal with such an employee is to
   A. ignore him, until he sees the error of his behavior
   B. frequently reassure him of his value as a person
   C. advise him that oversensitive people rarely get promoted
   D. issue written instructions to him to avoid misinterpretation

3.___

4. The understanding supervisor should recognize that a cer-   4.___
   tain amount of anxiety is common to all newly-hired employees.
   If you are a supervisor of a unit and a newly-hired em-
   ployee has been assigned to you, you can usually assume
   that the LEAST likely worry that the new employee has is
   worry about
   A. the job and the standards required in the job
   B. his acceptance by the other people in your unit
   C. the difficulty of advancing to top positions in
      the agency
   D. your fairness in evaluating his work

5. In assigning work to subordinates, it is often desirable   5.___
   for you to tell them the overall or ultimate objective
   of the assignment.
   Of the following, the BEST reason for telling them the
   objective is that it will
   A. assure them that you know what you are doing
   B. eliminate most of the possible complaints about
      the assignment
   C. give them confidence in their ability to do the
      assignment
   D. help them to make decisions consistent with the
      objective

6. Generally a supervisor wishes to increase the likelihood   6.___
   that instructions given to subordinates will be carried
   out properly.
   Of the following, the MOST important action for the super-
   visor to take to accomplish this objective when giving
   instructions to subordinates is to
   A. tailor the instructions to fit the interests of the
      subordinate
   B. use proper timing in giving the instruction
   C. make sure that the subordinates understand the in-
      structions
   D. include only those instructions that are essential
      to the task at hand

7. Suppose that a supervisor, because of his heavy workload,   7.___
   has decided to delegate to his subordinates some of the
   duties that he has been performing.
   Of the following attitudes of the supervisor, the one
   that is LEAST conducive toward effective delegation is
   his belief that
   A. his subordinates will make some mistakes in perform-
      ing these duties
   B. controls will be necessary to make sure the work is
      done
   C. performance of these duties may be slowed down
      temporarily
   D. much of his time will be spent supervising perform-
      ance of these duties

8. In attempting to determine why one of his subordinates   8.___
   has frequently been coming to work late, a supervisor
   begins an interview with the subordinate by asking her
   whether everything is all right on the job and at home.
   The BEST of the following reasons for beginning the interview in this manner is that a question specifically about
   the reason for the lateness
   A. might indicate insecurity on the part of the super-
      visor
   B. might limit the responses of the subordinate
   C. will offend the subordinate
   D. might reveal the purpose of the interview

9. Of the following, the BEST use to which a supervisor   9.___
   should put his knowledge of human relations is to
   A. enhance his image among his subordinates
   B. improve interpersonal relationships with the
      organization
   C. prompt the organization to an awareness of mental
      health
   D. resolve technical differences of opinion among
      employees

10. Which of the following types of information would come   10.___
    tribute LEAST to a measure of the quality of working
    conditions for employees in various jobs?
    A. Data reflecting a view of working conditions as
       seen through the eyes of workers
    B. Objective data relating to problems in working
       conditions, such as occupational safety statistics
    C. The considered opinion of recognized specialists in
       relevant fields
    D. The impressionistic accounts of journalists in
       feature articles

Questions 11 - 15.

DIRECTIONS: Questions 11 through 15 each consist of a sentence
              which may or may not be an example of good English
              usage. Consider grammar, punctuation, spelling,
              capitalization, verbosity, awkwardness, etc. Examine
              each sentence, and then choose the correct statement
              about it from the four choices below it. If the
              English usage in the sentence is better as given than
              with any of the changes suggested in options B, C, or
              D, choose option A. Do NOT choose an option that will
              change the meaning of the sentence.

11. The clerk could have completed the assignment on time   11.___
    if he knows where these materials were located.
    A. This is an example of acceptable writing.
    B. The word *knows* should be replaced by *had known*.
    C. The word *were* should be replaced by *had been*.
    D. The words *where these materials were located* should
       be replaced by *the location of these materials*.

12. All employees should be given safety training. Not just   12.____
    those who have accidents.
    A. This is an example of acceptable writing.
    B. The period after the word *training* should be
       changed to a colon.
    C. The period after the word *training* should be changed
       to a semicolon, and the first letter of the word *Not*
       should be changed to a small *n*.
    D. The period after the word *training* should be changed
       to a comma, and the first letter of the word *Not*
       should be changed to a small *n*.

13. This proposal is designed to promote employee awareness   13.____
    of the suggestion program, to encourage employee partici-
    pation in the program, and to increase the number of
    suggestions submitted.
    A. This is an example of acceptable writing.
    B. The word *proposal* should be spelled *preposal*.
    C. the words *to increase the number of suggestions
       submitted* should be changed to *an increase in the
       number of suggestions is expected*.
    D. The word *promote* should be changed to *enhance*
       and the word *increase* should be changed to *add
       to*.

14. The introduction of inovative managerial techniques   14.____
    should be preceded by careful analysis of the specific
    circumstances and conditions in each department.
    A. This is an example of acceptable writing.
    B. The word *techniques* should be spelled *techneques*.
    C. The word *inovative* should be spelled *innovative*.
    D. A comma should be placed after the word *circumstance*
       and after the word *conditions*.

15. This occurrence indicates that such criticism embarrasses   15.____
    him.
    A. This is an example of acceptable writing.
    B. The word *occurrence* should be spelled *occurence*.
    C. The word *criticism* should be spelled *criticizm*.
    D. The word *embarrasses* should be spelled *embarasses*.

Questions 16 - 18.

DIRECTIONS: Questions 16 through 18 each consist of four sentences.
               Choose the one sentence in each set of four that would
               be BEST for a *formal* letter or report. Consider grammar
               and appropriate usage.

16. A. Most all the work he completed before he become ill.   16.____
    B. He completed most of the work before becoming ill.
    C. Prior to him becoming ill his work was mostly com-
       pleted.
    D. Before he became ill most of the work he had completed.

17. A. Being that the report lacked a clearly worded recom-   17.___
       mendation, it did not matter that it contained enough
       information.
    B. There was enough information in the report, although
       it, including the recommendation, were not clearly
       worded.
    C. Although the report contained enough information, it
       did not have a clearly worded recommendation.
    D. Though the report did not have a recommendation that
       was clearly worded, and the information therein con-
       tained was enough.

18. A. Having already overlooked the important mistakes,   18.___
       the ones which she found were not as important to-
       ward the end of the letter.
    B. Toward the end of the letter she had already over-
       looked the important mistakes, so that which she had
       found were not as important.
    C. The mistakes which she had already overlooked were
       not as important as those which near the end of letter
       she had found.
    D. The mistakes which she found near the end of the let-
       ter were not as important as those which she had al-
       ready overlooked.

19. Examine the following sentence, and then choose from   19.___
    below the words which should be inserted in the blank
    spaces to produce the best sentence.
       The unit has exceeded _____ goals and the employees
       are satisfied with _____ accomplishments.
       A. their, it's   B. it's, it's
       C. its, there   D. its, their

20. Examine the following sentence, and then choose from   20.___
    below the words which should be inserted in the blank
    spaces to produce the best sentence.
       Research indicates that employees who _____ no op-
       portunity for close social relationships often find
       their work unsatisfying, and this _____ of satisfac-
       tion often reflects itself in low production.
       A. have, lack   B. have, excess
       B. has, lack   D. has, excess

KEY (CORRECT ANSWERS)

1. A	6. C	11. B	16. B
2. C	7. D	12. D	17. C
3. B	8. B	13. A	18. D
4. C	9. B	14. C	19. D
5. D	10. D	15. A	20. A

TEST 2

DIRECTIONS: Each question or incomplete statement is followed by several suggested answers or completions. Select the one that BEST answers the question or completes the statement. *PRINT THE LETTER OF THE CORRECT ANSWER IN THE SPACE AT THE RIGHT.*

1. Of the following, the GREATEST *pitfall* in interviewing is that the result may be effected by the
   A. bias of the interviewee
   B. bias of the interviewer
   C. educational level of the interviewee
   D. educational level of the interviewer

   1.___

2. Assume that you have been asked to interview each of several students who have been hired to work part-time. Which of the following could *ordinarily* be accomplished LEAST effectively in such an interview?
   A. Providing information about the organization or institution in which the students will be working
   B. Directing the students to report for work each afternoon at specified times
   C. Determining experience and background of the students so that appropriate assignments can be made
   D. Changing the attitudes of the students toward the importance of parental controls

   2.___

3. Assume that someone you are interviewing is reluctant to give you certain information.
   He would *probably* be MORE responsive if you show him that
   A. all the other persons you interviewed provided you with the information
   B. it would serve his own best interests to give you the information
   C. the information is very important to you
   D. you are businesslike and take a no-nonsense approach

   3.___

4. Taking notes while you are interviewing someone is *most likely* to
   A. arouse doubts as to your trustworthiness
   B. give the interviewee confidence in your ability
   C. insure that you record the facts you think are important
   D. make the responses of the interviewee unreliable

   4.___

5. Assume that you have been asked to get all the pertinent information from an employee who claims that she witnessed a robbery.
   Which of the following questions is LEAST likely to influence the witness's response?
   A. *Can you describe the robber's hair?*
   B. *Did the robber have a lot of hair?*
   C. *Was the robber's hair black or brown?*
   D. *Was the robber's hair very dark?*

   5.___

6. If you are to interview several applicants for jobs and   6.___
rate them on five different factors on a scale of 1 to
5, you should be MOST careful to *insure* that your
   A. rating on one factor does not influence your rating
   on another factor
   B. ratings on all factors are interrelated with a
   minimum of variation
   C. overall evaluation for employment exactly reflects
   the arithmetic average of your ratings
   D. overall evaluation for employment is unrelated to
   your individual ratings

7. In answering questions asked by students, faculty, and   7.___
the public, it is MOST important that
   A. you indicate your source of information
   B. you are not held responsible for the answers
   C. the facts you give be accurate
   D. the answers cover every possible aspect of each
   question

8. One of the applicants for a menial job is a tall, stooped, 8.___
husky individual with a low forehead, narrow eyes, a pro-
truding chin, and a tendency to keep his mouth open.
In interviewing him, you *should*
   A. check him more carefully than the other applicants
   regarding criminal background
   B. disregard any skills he might have for other jobs
   which are vacant
   C. make your vocabulary somewhat simpler than with the
   other applicants
   D. make no assumption regarding his ability on the
   basis of his appearance

9. Of the following, the BEST approach for you to use at   9.___
the beginning of an interview with a job applicant is to
   A. caution him to use his time economically and to get
   to the point
   B. ask him how long he intends to remain on the job if
   hired
   C. make some pleasant remarks to put him at ease
   D. emphasize the importance of the interview in obtaining the job

10. Of the following, the BEST reason for conducting an   10.___
exit interview with an employee is to
   A. make certain that he returns all identification
   cards and office keys
   B. find out why he is leaving
   C. provide a useful training device for the exit
   interviewer
   D. discover if his initial hiring was in error

11. Suppose that a visitor to an office asks a receptionist
    for a specific person by name. The person is available,
    but the visitor refuses to state the purpose of the visit,
    saying that it is *personal*.
    Which of the following is the MOST appropriate response
    for the receptionist to make?
    A. *Does M_____ know you?*
    B. *I'm sorry, M_____ is busy.*
    C. *M____ won't be able to help you unless you're
       more specific.*
    D. *M____ is not able to see you.*

11.___

12. When writing a reply to a letter you received, it is
    proper to mention the subject of the letter.
    However, you should ordinarily NOT summarize the contents
    or repeat statements made in the letter you received PRI-
    MARILY because
    A. a letter writer answers people, not letters
    B. direct answers will help you avoid sounding pompous
    C. the response will thus be more confidential
    D. the sender usually knows what he or she wrote

12.___

13. Assume that you are a supervisor in an office which gets
    approximately equal quantities of urgent work and work
    that is not urgent. The volume of work is high during
    some periods and low during others.
    In order to level out the fluctuations in workload, it
    would be BEST for you to schedule work so that
    A. urgent work which comes up in a period of high work
       volume can be handled expeditiously by the use of
       voluntary overtime
    B. urgent work is postponed for completion in periods
       of low volume
    C. work is completed as it comes into the office, ex-
       cept that when urgent work arises, other work is
       laid aside temporarily
    D. work is completed chronologically, that is, on the
       basis of *first in, first out*

13.___

14. Suppose that a supervisor sets up a pick-up and delivery
    messenger system to cover several nearby buildings. Each
    building has at least one station for both pick-up and
    delivery. Three messenger trips are scheduled for each
    day, and the messenger is instructed to make pick-ups
    and deliveries at the same time.
    In this situation, telling the messenger to visit each
    pick-up and delivery station even though there is noth-
    ing to deliver to it is
    A. *advisable*, messengers are generally not capable of
       making decisions for themselves
    B. *advisable*, there may be material for the messenger
       to pick up
    C. *inadvisable*, the system must be made flexible to
       meet variable workload conditions
    D. *inadvisable*, postponing the visit until there is
       something to deliver is more efficient

14.___

15. You, as a unit head, have been asked to submit budget   15.___
    estimates of staff, equipment and supplies in terms of
    programs for your unit for the coming fiscal year.
    In addition to their use in planning, such unit budget
    estimates can be BEST used to
    A. reveal excessive costs in operations
    B. justify increases in+the debt limit
    C. analyze employee salary adjustments
    D. predict the success of future programs

Questions 16 - 21.

DIRECTIONS: Questions 16 through 21 involve calculations of annual
             grade averages for college students who have just com-
             pleted their junior year. These averages are to be
             based on the following table showing the number of
             credit hours for each student during the year at each
             of the grade levels: A, B, C, D, and F. How these
             letter grades may be translated into numerical grades
             is indicated in the first column of the table.

Grade Value	Credit Hours - Junior Year					
	King	Lewis	Martin	Nonkin	Ottly	Perry
A = 95	12	12	9	15	6	3
B = 85	9	12	9	12	18	6
C = 75	6	6	9	3	3	21
D = 65	3	3	3	3	–	–
F = 0	–	–	3	–	–	–

    Calculating a grade average for an individual student is a 4-
step process:
    I. Multiply each grade value by the number of credit hours
       for which the student received that grade.
   II. Add these multiplication products for each student.
  III. Add the student's total credit hours.
   IV. Divide the multiplication product total by the total
       number of credit hours.
    V. Round the result, if there is a decimal place, to the
       nearest whole number. A number ending in .5 would be
       rounded to the next higher number.

EXAMPLE

Using student King's grades as an example, his grade average can be calculated by going through the following four steps:

I. 95 x 12 = 1140   III. 12
    85 x)9 = 765   9
    75 x 6 = 450   6
    65 x 3 = 195   3
     0 x 0 =   0   0
                              ──── 30 TOTAL credit hours
II. TOTAL   = 2550

IV. Divide 2550 by 30: $\frac{2550}{30} = 85$.

King's grade average is 85.

Answer Questions 16 through 21 on the basis of the information given above.

16. The grade average of Lewis is
    A. 83   B. 84   C. 85   D. 86   16.____

17. The grade average of Martin is
    A. 72   B. 73   C. 74   D. 75   17.____

18. The grade average of Nonkin is
    A. 85   B. 86   C. 87   D. 88   18.____

19. Student Ottly must attain a grade average of 90 in each   19.____
    of his years in college to be accepted into the graduate
    school of his choice.
    If, in summer school during his junior year, he takes two
    3-credit courses and receives a grade of 95 in each one, his
    grade average for his junior year will then be, *most nearly*,
    A. 87   B. 88   C. 89   D. 90

20. If Perry takes an additional 3-credit course during the   20.____
    year and receives a grade of 95, his grade average will
    be increased to approximately
    A. 79   B. 80   C. 81   D. 82

21. What has been the *effect* of automation in data process-   21.____
    ing on the planning of manageráal objectives?
    A. Paperwork can be virtually eliminated from the
       planning process.
    B. The information on which such planning is based
       can be more precise and up-to-date.
    C. Planning must be done much more frequently because
       of the constantly changing nature of the objectives.
    D. Planning can be done much less frequently because
       of the increased stability of objectives.

22. Which of the following is the BEST reason for budgeting   22.___
    a new calculating machine for an office?
    A. The clerks in the office often make mistakes in
       adding.
    B. The machine would save time and money.
    C. It was budgeted last year but never received.
    D. All the other offices have calculating machines.

23. Which of the following is *most likely* to reduce the   23.___
    volume of paperwork in a unit responsible for preparing
    a large number of reports?
    A. Changing the office layout so that there will be
       a minimum of backtracking and delay.
    B. Acquiring additional adding and calculating machines.
    C. Consolidating some of the reports.
    D. Inaugurating a *records retention* policy to reduce
       the length of time office papers are retained.

24. With regard to typed correspondence received by most   24.___
    offices, which of the following is the GREATEST problem?
    A. Verbosity   B. Illegibility
    C. Improper folding   D. Excessive copies

25. Of the following, the GREATEST advantage of electronic   25.___
    typewriters over electric typewriters is that they *usual-
    ly*
    A. are less expensive to repair
    B. are smaller and lighter
    C. produce better looking copy
    D. require less training for the typist

KEY (CORRECT ANSWERS)

1. B	6. A	11. A	16. C	21. B
2. D	7. C	12. D	17. D	22. B
3. B	8. D	13. C	18. C	23. C
4. C	9. C	14. B	19. B	24. A
5. A	10. B	15. A	20. B	25. C

EXAMINATION SECTION
TEST 1

DIRECTIONS: Each question or incomplete statement is followed by several suggested answers or completions. Select the one that BEST answers the question or completes the statement. *PRINT THE LETTER OF THE CORRECT ANSWER IN THE SPACE AT THE RIGHT.*

1. Records of one type or another are kept in every office. 1.___
   The MOST important of the following reasons for the supervisor of a clerical or stenographic unit to keep statistical records of the work done in his unit is generally to
   A. supply basic information needed in planning the work of the unit
   B. obtain statistics for comparison with other units
   C. serve as the basis for unsatisfactory employee evaluation
   D. provide the basis for special research projects on program budgeting

2. It is better for an employee to report and be responsible 2.___
   directly to several supervisors than to report and be responsible to only one supervisor.
   This statement directly CONTRADICTS the supervisory principle generally known as
   A. span of control   B. unity of command
   C. delegation of authority D. accountability

3. The one of the following which would MOST likely lead to 3.___
   friction among clerks in a unit is for the unit supervisor to
   A. defend the actions of his clerks when discussing them with his own supervisor
   B. praise each of his clerks *in confidence* as the best clerk in the unit
   C. get his men to work together as a team in completing the work of the unit
   D. consider the point of view of the rank and file clerks when assigning unpleasant tasks

4. You become aware that one of the employees you supervise 4.___
   has failed to follow correct procedure and has been permitting various reports to be prepared, typed, and transmitted improperly.
   The BEST action for you to take FIRST in this situation is to
   A. order the employee to review all departmental procedures and reprimand him for having violated them
   B. warn the employee that he must obey regulations because uniformity is essential for effective departmental operation

C. confer with the employee both about his failure to
   follow regulations and his reasons for doing so
D. watch the employee's work very closely in the future
   but say nothing about this violation

5. The supervisory clerk who would be MOST likely to have
   poor control over his subordinates is the one who
   A. goes to unusually great lengths to try to win their
      approval
   B. pitches in with the work they are doing during
      periods of heavy workload when no extra help can be
      obtained
   C. encourages and helps his subordinates toward advance-
      ment
   D. considers suggestions from his subordinates before
      establishing new work procedures involving them

5.____

6. Suppose that a clerk who has been transferred to your
   office from another division in your agency because of
   difficulties with his supervisor has been placed under
   your supervision.
   The BEST course of action for you to take FIRST is to
   A. instruct the clerk in the duties he will be per-
      forming in your office and make him feel *wanted* in
      his new position
   B. analyze the clerk's past grievance to determine if
      the transfer was the best solution to the problem
   C. advise him of the difficulties his former super-
      visor had with other employees and encourage him
      not to feel bad about the transfer
   D. warn him that you will not tolerate any nonsense
      and that he will be under continuous surveillance
      while assigned to you

6.____

7. A certain office supervisor takes the initiative to
   represent his employees' interests related to working
   conditions, opportunities for advancement, etc. to his
   own supervisor and the administrative levels of the
   agency.
   This supervisor's actions will MOST probably have the
   effect of
   A. preventing employees from developing individual
      initiative in their work goals
   B. encouraging employees to compete openly for the
      special attention of their supervisor
   C. depriving employees of the opportunity to be
      represented by persons and/or unions of their own
      choosing
   D. building employee confidence in their supervisor
      and a spirit of cooperation in their work

7.____

8. Suppose that you have been promoted, assigned as a super-   8.___
   visor of a certain unit, and asked to reorganize its
   functions so that specific routine procedures can be
   established.
   Before deciding which routines to establish, the FIRST
   of the following steps you should take is to
       A. decide who will perform each task in the routine
       B. determine the purpose to be served by each routine
          procedure
       C. outline the sequence of steps in each routine to be
          established
       D. calculate if more staff will be needed to carry out
          the new procedures

9. When routine procedures covering the ordinary work of an   9.___
   office are established, the supervisor of the office tends
   to be relieved of the need to
       A. make repeated decisions on the handling of recurring
          similar situations
       B. check the accuracy of the work completed by his
          subordinates
       C. train his subordinates in new work procedures
       D. plan and schedule the work of his office

10. Of the following, the method which would be LEAST help-   10.___
    ful to a supervisor in effectively applying the princi-
    ples of on-the-job safety to the daily work of his unit
    is for him to
       A. initiate corrections of unsafe layouts of equipment
          and unsafe work processes
       B. take charge of operations that are not routine to
          make certain that safety precautions are established
          and observed
       C. continue to *talk safety* and promote safety conscious-
          ness in his subordinates
       D. figure the cost of all accidents which could possi-
          bly occur on the job

11. A clerk is assigned to serve as receptionist for a large   11.___
    and busy office. Although many members of the public
    visit this office, the clerk often experiences periods
    of time in which he has nothing to do.
    In these circumstances, the MOST advisable of the
    following actions for the supervisor to take is to
       A. assign a number of relatively low priority clerical
          jobs to the receptionist to do in the slow periods
       B. regularly rotate this assignment so that all of the
          clerks experience this lighter work load
       C. assign the receptionist job as part of the duties
          of a number of clerks whose desks are nearest the
          reception room
       D. overlook the situation since most of the recep-
          tionist's time is spent in performing a necessary
          and meaningful function

12. For a supervisor to require all stenographers in a stenographic pool to produce the same amount of work on a particular day is

    A. *advisable* since it will prove that the supervisor plays no favorites

    B. *fair* since all the stenographers are receiving approximately the same salary, their output should be equivalent

    C. *not necessary* since the fast workers will compensate for the slow workers

    D. *not realistic* since individual differences in abilities and work assignment must be taken into consideration

12.____

13. The establishment of a centralized typing pool to service the various units in an organization is MOST likely to be worthwhile when there is

    A. wide fluctuation from time to time in the needs of the various units for typing service

    B. a large volume of typing work to be done in each of the units

    C. a need by each unit for different kinds of typing service

    D. a training program in operation to develop and maintain typing skills

13.____

14. A newly appointed supervisor should learn as much as possible about the backgrounds of his subordinates. This statement is GENERALLY correct because

    A. knowing their backgrounds assures they will be treated objectively, equally, and without favor

    B. effective handling of subordinates is based upon knowledge of their individual differences

    C. subordinates perform more efficiently under one supervisor than under another

    D. subordinates have confidence in a supervisor who knows all about them

14.____

15. The use of electronic computers in modern businesses has produced many changes in office and information management.
Of the following, it would NOT be correct to state that computer utilization

    A. broadens the scope of managerial and supervisory authority

    B. establishes uniformity in the processing and reporting of information

    C. cuts costs by reducing the personnel needed for efficient office operation

    D. supplies management rapidly with up-to-date data to facilitate decision-making

15.____

16. The CHIEF advantage of having a single, large open   16.___
     office instead of small partitioned ones for a clerical
     unit or stenographic pool is that the single, large
     open office
        A. affords privacy without isolation for all office
           workers not directly dealing with the public
        B. assures the smoother, more continuous inter-office
           flow of work that is essential for efficient work
           production
        C. facilitates the office supervisor's visual control
           over and communication with his subordinates
        D. permits a more decorative and functional arrangement
           of office furniture and machines

17. When a supervisor provides a new employee with the infor-   17.___
     mation necessary for a basic knowledge and a general
     understanding of practices and procedures of the agency,
     he is applying the type of training generally known as
     _____ training.
        A. pre-employment   B. induction
        C. on-the-job   D. supervisory

18. Many government agencies require the approval by a   18.___
     central forms control unit of the design and reproduction
     of new office forms.
     The one of the following results of this procedure that
     is a DISADVANTAGE is that requiring prior approval of a
     central forms control unit usually
        A. limits the distribution of forms to those offices
           with justifiable reasons for receiving them
        B. permits checking whether existing forms or modifi-
           cations of them are in line with current agency
           needs
        C. encourages reliance on only the central office to
           set up all additional forms when needed
        D. provides for someone with a specialized knowledge
           of forms design to review and criticize new and
           revised forms

19. Suppose that a large quantity of information is in the   19.___
     files which are located a good distance from your desk.
     Almost every worker in your office must use these files
     constantly. Your duties in particular require that you
     daily refer to about 25 of the same items. They are
     short, one-page items distributed throughout the files.
     In this situation, your BEST course would be to
        A. take the items that you use daily from the files
           and keep them on your desk, inserting *out cards*
           in their place
        B. go to the files each time you need the information
           so that the items will be there when other workers
           need them
        C. make xerox copies of the information you use most
           frequently and keep them in your desk for ready
           reference

D. label the items you use most often with different colored tabs for immediate identification

20. Of the following, the MOST important advantage of pre-paring manuals of office procedures in loose-leaf form is that this form
    A. permits several employees to use different sections simultaneously
    B. facilitates the addition of new material and the removal of obsolete material
    C. is more readily arranged in alphabetical order
    D. reduces the need for cross-references to locate material carried under several headings

20.____

21. Suppose that you establish a new clerical procedure for the unit you supervise. Your keeping a close check on the time required by your staff to handle the new procedure is WISE mainly because such a check will find out
    A. whether your subordinates know how to handle the new procedure
    B. whether a revision of the unit's work schedule will be necessary as a result of the new procedure
    C. what attitude your employees have toward the new procedure
    D. what alterations in job descriptions will be necessitated by the new procedure

21.____

22. From the viewpoint of an office supervisor, the BEST of the following reasons for distributing the incoming mail before the beginning of the regular work day is that
    A. distribution can be handled quickly and most efficiently at that time
    B. distribution later in the day may be distracting to or interfere with other employees
    C. the employees who distribute the mail can then perform other tasks during the rest of the day
    D. office activities for the day based on the mail may then be started promptly

22.____

23. Suppose you are the head of a unit with 10 staff members who are located in several different rooms.
If you want to inform your staff of a minor change in procedure, the BEST and LEAST expensive way of doing so would usually be to
    A. send a mimeographed copy to each staff member
    B. call a special staff meeting and announce the change
    C. circulate a memo, having each staff member initial it
    D. have a clerk tell each member of the staff about the change

23.____

24. The numbered statements below relate to the stenographic   24.___
    skill of taking dictation. According to authorities on
    secretarial practices, which of these are generally
    recommended guides to development of efficient steno-
    graphic skills?
      I. A stenographer should date her notebook daily to
         facilitate locating certain notes at a later time.
     II. A stenographer should make corrections of gramma-
         tical mistakes while her boss is dictating to her.
    III. A stenographer should draw a line through the
         dictated matter in her notebook after she has
         transcribed it.
     IV. A stenographer should write in longhand unfamiliar
         names and addresses dictated to her.

    The CORRECT answer is:
      A. Only Statements I, II, and III are generally
         recommended guides.
      B. Only Statements II, III, and IV are generally
         recommended guides.
      C. Only Statements I, III, and IV are generally
         recommended guides.
      D. All four statements are generally recommended guides.

25. A bureau of a city agency is about to move to a new   25.___
    location.
    Of the following, the FIRST step that should be taken
    in order to provide a good layout for the office at the
    new location is to
      A. decide the exact amount of space to be assigned to
         each unit of the bureau
      B. decide whether to lay out a single large open office
         or one consisting of small partitioned units
      C. ask each unit chief in the bureau to examine the
         new location and submit a request for the amount of
         space he needs
      D. prepare a detailed plan of the dimensions of the
         floor space to be occupied by the bureau at the new
         location

26. Of the following, the BEST reason for discarding a sheet   26.___
    of carbon paper is that
      A. some carbon rubs off on your fingers when handled
      B. there are several creases in the sheet
      C. the short edge of the sheet is curled
      D. the finish on the sheet is smooth and shiny

27. Suppose you are the supervisor of the mailroom of a   27.___
    large city agency where the mail received daily is opened
    by machine, sorted by hand for delivery, and time-stamped.
    Letters and any enclosures are removed from envelopes and
    stapled together before distribution. One of your newest
    clerks asks you what should be done when a letter makes
    reference to an enclosure, but no enclosure is in the
    envelope.

You should tell him that, in this situation, the BEST procedure is to
A. make an entry of the sender's name and address in the *missing enclosures* file and forward the letter to its proper destination
B. return the letter to its sender, attaching a request for the missing enclosure
C. put the letter aside until a proper investigation may be made concerning the missing enclosure
D. route the letter to the person for whom it is intended, noting the absence of the enclosure on the letter-margin

28. The term *work flow*, when used in connection with office management or the activities in an office, GENERALLY means the
A. use of charts in the analysis of various office functions
B. rate of speed at which work flows through a single section of an office
C. step-by-step physical routing of work through its various procedures
D. number of individual work units which can be produced by the average employee

28.___

29. Physical conditions can have a definite effect on the efficiency and morale of an office.
Which of the following statements about physical conditions in an office is CORRECT?
A. Hard, non-porous surfaces reflect more noise than linoleum on the top of a desk.
B. Painting in tints of bright yellow is more appropriate for sunny, well-lit offices than for dark, poorly-lit offices.
C. Plate glass is better than linoleum for the top of a desk.
D. The central typing room needs less light than a conference room does.

29.___

30. In a certain filing system, documents are consecutively numbered as they are filed, a register is maintained of such consecutively numbered documents, and a record is kept of the number of each document removed from the files and its destination.
This system will NOT help in
A. finding the present whereabouts of a particular document
B. proving the accuracy of the data recorded on a certain document
C. indicating whether observed existing documents were ever filed
D. locating a desired document without knowing what its contents are

30.___

31. In deciding the kind and number of records an agency   31.___
    should keep, the administrative staff must recognize
    that records are of value in office management PRIMARILY
    as
    A. informational bases for agency activities
    B. data for evaluating the effectiveness of the agency
    C. raw material on which statistical analyses are to
       be based
    D. evidence that the agency is carrying out its duties
       and responsibilities

32. Complaints are often made by the public about the   32.___
    government's procedures. Although in most cases such
    procedures cannot be changed since various laws and
    regulations require them, it may still be possible to
    reduce the number of complaints.
    Which one of the following actions by personnel dealing
    with applicants for city services is LEAST likely to
    reduce complaints concerning city procedures?
    A. Treating all citizens alike and explaining to them
       that no exceptions to required procedures can be
       made
    B. Explaining briefly to the citizen why he should
       comply with regulations
    C. Being careful to avoid mistakes which may make
       additional interviews or correspondence necessary
    D. Keeping the citizen informed of the progress of his
       correspondence when immediate disposition cannot be
       made

33. Persons whose native language is not English sometimes   33.___
    experience difficulty in communication when visiting
    public offices.
    The MOST common method used by such persons to overcome
    the difficulty in communication is to
    A. write in their own language whatever they wish to say
    B. hire a professional interpreter
    C. ask a patrolman for assistance
    D. bring with them an English-speaking friend or relative

34. In answering a complaint made by a member of the public 34.___
    that a certain essential procedure required by your
    agency is difficult to follow, it would be BEST for you
    to stress most
    A. that a change in the rules may be considered if
       enough complaints are received
    B. why the operation of a large agency sometimes proves
       a hardship in individual cases
    C. the necessity for the procedure
    D. the origin of the procedure

35. When talking to a citizen, it is BEST for an employee of   35. ____
     government to
        A. use ordinary conversational phrases and a natural
           manner
        B. try to copy the pronunciation and level of education
           shown by the citizen
        C. try to speak in a very cultured manner and tone
        D. use technical terms to show his familiarity with
           his own work

36. Employees who service the public should maintain an   36. ____
     attitude which is both sympathetic and objective.
     An unsympathetic and subjective attitude would be shown
     by a public employee who
        A. says *no* with a smile when a citizen's request must
           be denied
        B. listens attentively to a long complaint from a
           citizen about government's *red tape*
        C. responds with sarcasm when a citizen asks a question
           which has an obvious manner
        D. suggests a definite solution to a citizen's problems

37. Of the following methods of conducting an interview,   37. ____
     the BEST is to
        A. ask questions with *yes* or *no* answers
        B. listen carefully and ask only questions that are
           pertinent
        C. fire questions at the interviewee so that he must
           answer sincerely and briefly
        D. read standardized questions to the person being
           interviewed

38. An interviewer should begin with topics which are easy   38. ____
     to talk about and which are not threatening.
     This procedure is useful MAINLY because it
        A. allows the applicant a little time to get accustomed
           to the situation and leads to freer communication
        B. distracts the attention of the person being inter-
           viewed from the main purpose of the questioning
        C. is the best way for the interviewer to show that he
           is relaxed and confident on the job
        D. causes the interviewee to feel that the interviewer
           is apportioning valuable questioning time

39. The initial interview will normally be more of a problem   39. ____
     to the interviewer than any subsequent interviews he may
     have with the same person because
        A. the interviewee is likely to be hostile
        B. there is too much to be accomplished in one session
        C. he has less information about the client than he
           will have later
        D. some information may be forgotten when later making
           record of this first interview

40. You are a supervisor in an agency and are holding your   40.___
    first interview with a new employee.
    In this interview, you should strive MAINLY to
        A. show the new employee that you are an efficient and
           objective supervisor, with a completely impersonal
           attitude toward your subordinate
        B. complete the entire orientation process including
           the giving of detailed job-duty instructions
        C. make it clear to the employee that all your deci-
           sions are based on your many years of experience
        D. lay the groundwork for a good employee-supervisor
           relationship by gaining the new employee's confidence

41. Most successful interviews are those in which the inter-   41.___
    viewer shows a genuine interest in the person he is
    questioning.
    This attitude would MOST likely cause the individual
    being interviewed to
        A. feel that the interviewer already knows all the facts
           in his case
        B. act more naturally and reveal more of his true
           feelings
        C. request that the interviewer give more attention to
           his problems, not his personality
        D. react defensively, suppress his negative feelings,
           and conceal the real facts in his case

42. Questions worded so that the person being interviewed   42.___
    has some hint of the desired answer can modify the
    person's response.
    The result of the inclusion of such questions in an
    interview, even when they are used inadvertently, is to
        A. have no effect on the basic content of the informa-
           tion given by the person interviewed
        B. have value in convincing the person that the
           suggested plan is the best for him
        C. cause the person to give more meaningful informa-
           tion
        D. reduce the validity of the information obtained
           from the person

43. The person MOST likely to be a good interviewer is one   43.___
    who
        A. is able to outguess the person being interviewed
        B. tries to change the attitudes of the persons he
           interviews
        C. controls the interview by skillfully dominating
           the conversation
        D. is able to imagine himself in the position of the
           person being interviewed

44. The *halo effect* is an overall impression on the inter-
    viewer, whether favorable or unfavorable, usually created
    by a single trait. This impression then influences the
    appraisal of all other factors.
    A *halo effect* is LEAST likely to be created at an inter-
    view where the interviewee is a
    A. person of average appearance and ability
    B. rough-looking man who uses abusive language
    C. young attractive woman being interviewed by a man
    D. person who demonstrates an exceptional ability to
       remember facts

44. ____

45. Of the following, the BEST way for an interviewer to
    calm a person who seems to have become emotionally upset
    as a result of a question asked is for the interviewer to
    A. talk to the person about other things for a short
       time
    B. ask that the person control himself
    C. probe for the cause of his emotional upset
    D. finish the questioning as quickly as possible

45. ____

46. Of the following, a centralized filing system is LEAST
    suitable for filing
    A. material which is confidential in nature
    B. routine correspondence
    C. periodic reports of the divisions of the department
    D. material used by several divisions of the department

46. ____

47. Form letters should be used MAINLY when
    A. an office has to reply to a great many similar
       inquiries
    B. the type of correspondence varies widely
    C. it is necessary to have letters which are well-
       phrased and grammatically correct
    D. letters of inquiry have to be answered as soon as
       possible after they are received

47. ____

48. Suppose that you are assigned to prepare a form from
    which certain information will be posted in a ledger.
    It would be MOST helpful to the person posting the
    information in the ledger if, in designing the form,
    you were to
    A. use the same color paper for both the form and the
       ledger
    B. make the form the same size as the pages of the
       ledger
    C. have the information on the form in the same order
       as that used in the ledger
    D. include in the form a box which is to be initialed
       when the data on the form have been posted in the
       ledger

48. ____

49. A misplaced record is a lost record.
    Of the following, the MOST valid implication of this
    statement in regard to office work is that
    A. all records in an office should be filed in strict
       alphabetical order
    B. accuracy in filing is essential
    C. only one method of filing should be used throughout
       the office
    D. files should be locked when not in use

49.___

50. James Jones is applying for a provisional appointment as
    a clerk in your department. He presents a letter of
    recommendation from a former employer stating: *James
    Jones was rarely late or absent; he has a very pleasing
    manner and never got into an argument with his fellow
    employees.*
    The above information concerning this applicant
    A. proves clearly that he produces more work than the
       average employee
    B. indicates that he was probably attempting to con-
       ceal his inefficiency from his former employer
    C. presents no conclusive evidence of his ability to
       do clerical work
    D. indicates clearly that with additional training he
       will make a good supervisor

50.___

KEY (CORRECT ANSWERS)

1. A	11. A	21. B	31. A	41. B
2. B	12. D	22. D	32. A	42. D
3. B	13. A	23. C	33. D	43. D
4. C	14. B	24. C	34. C	44. A
5. A	15. A	25. D	35. A	45. A
6. A	16. C	26. B	36. C	46. A
7. D	17. B	27. D	37. B	47. A
8. B	18. C	28. C	38. A	48. C
9. A	19. C	29. A	39. C	49. B
10. D	20. B	30. B	40. D	50. C

TEST 2

DIRECTIONS: Each question or incomplete statement is followed by several suggested answers or completions. Select the one that BEST answers the question or completes the statement. *PRINT THE LETTER OF THE CORRECT ANSWER IN THE SPACE AT THE RIGHT.*

Questions 1-10.

DIRECTIONS: In each Question 1 through 10, there is a quotation which contains a word (one of those underlined) that is either incorrectly used because it is not in keeping with the meaning the quotation is evidently intended to convey, or is misspelled. There is only one incorrect word in each quotation. Of the four underlined words in each question, determine if the first one should be replaced by the word lettered A, the second replaced by the word lettered B, the third replaced by the word lettered C, or the fourth replaced by the word lettered D. Print the letter of the replacement word you have selected in the space at the right.

1. Whether one depends on flourescent or artificial light or both, adequate standards should be maintained by means of systematic tests.   1.____
   A. natural   B. safeguards
   C. established   D. routine

2. A policeman has to be prepared to assume his knowledge as a social scientist in the community.   2.____
   A. forced   B. role
   C. philosopher   D. street

3. It is practically impossible to tell whether a sentence is very long simply by measuring its length.   3.____
   A. almost   B. mark   C. too   D. denoting

4. By using carbon paper, the typist easily is able to insert as many as six copies of a report.   4.____
   A. adding   B. seldom   C. make   D. forms

5. Although all people have many traits in common, a receptionist in her agreements with people learns quickly how different each person is from every other person.   5.____
   A. impressions   B. associations
   C. decides   D. various

6. Strong leaders are required to organize a community for delinquency prevention and for dissemination of organized crime and drug addiction.   6.____
   A. tactics   B. important   C. control   D. meetings

7. The demonstrators, who were taken to the Criminal Courts   7.___
   building in Manhattan (because it was large enough to
   accommodate them), contended that the arrests were
   unwarrented.
       A. demonstraters   B. Manhatten
       C. accomodate   D. unwarranted

8. When two or more forms for spelling a word exist, it is   8.___
   advisable to use the preferred spelling indicated in the
   dictionary, and to use it consistantly.
       A. adviseable   B. prefered
       C. dictionery   D. consistently

9. If you know the language of the foreign country you are   9.___
   visiting, your embarassment will disappear and you will
   learn a lot more about the customs and characteristics
   of the common people.
       A. foriegn   B. embarrassment
       C. dissappear   D. charactaristics

10. Material consisting of government bulletins, advertice-   10.___
    ments, catalogues, announcements of address changes and
    any other periodical material of this nature, may be
    filed alphabetically according to subject.
        A. advertisements   B. cataloges
        C. periodicle   D. alphabeticly

Questions 11-14.

DIRECTIONS: Each of the two sentences in Questions 11 through 14
                  may contain errors in punctuation, capitalization, or
                  grammar.

                  If there is an error in only Sentence I, mark your
                  answer A.
                  If there is an error in only Sentence II, mark your
                  answer B.
                  If there is an error in both Sentences I and II, mark
                  your answer C.
                  If both Sentences I and II are correct, mark your
                  answer D.

11.   I. It is very annoying to have a pencil sharpener,   11.___
       which is not in proper working order.
    II. The building watchman checked the door of Charlie's
       office and found that the lock has been jammed.

12.   I. Since he went on the New York City council a year   12.___
       ago, one of his primary concerns has been safety
       in the streets.
    II. After waiting in the doorway for about 15 minutes,
       a black sedan appeared.

13. I. When you are studying a good textbook is important. 13.___
     II. He said he would divide the money equally between
         you and me.

14. I. The question is, "How can a large number of envelopes 14.___
         be sealed rapidly without the use of a sealing
         machine?"
     II. The administrator assigned two stenographers, Mary
         and I, to the new bureau.

Questions 15-16.

DIRECTIONS: In each of Questions 15 and 16, the four sentences are
             from a paragraph in a report. They are not in the right
             order. Which of the following arrangements is the BEST
             one?

15. 1. An executive may answer a letter by writing his reply 15.___
        on the face of the letter itself instead of having
        a return letter typed.
     2. This procedure is efficient because it saves the
        executive's time, the typist's time, and saves office
        file space.
     3. Copying machines are used in small offices as well as
        large offices to save time and money in making brief
        replies to business letters.
     4. A copy is made on a copying machine to go into the
        company files, while the original is mailed back to
        the sender.

     The CORRECT answer is:
        A. 1, 2, 4, 3   B. 1, 4, 2, 3
        C. 3, 1, 4, 2   D. 3, 4, 2, 1

16. 1. Most organizations favor one of the types but always 16.___
        include the others to a lesser degree.
     2. However, we can detect a definite trend toward
        greater use of symbolic control.
     3. We suggest that our local police agencies are today
        primarily utilizing material control.
     4. Control can be classified into three types: physical,
        material, and symbolic.

     The CORRECT answer is:
        A. 4, 2, 3, 1   B. 2, 1, 4, 3
        C. 3, 4, 2, 1   D. 4, 1, 3, 2

17. Of the following, the MOST effective report writing   17.___
     style is usually characterized by
        A. covering all the main ideas in the same paragraph
        B. presenting each significant point in a new paragraph
        C. placing the least important points before the most
           important points
        D. giving all points equal emphasis throughout the
           report

18. Of the following, which factor is COMMON to all types of reports?   18.___
    A. Presentation of information
    B. Interpretation of findings
    C. Chronological ordering of the information
    D. Presentation of conclusions and recommendations

19. When writing a report, the one of the following which you should do FIRST is   19.___
    A. set up a logical work schedule
    B. determine your objectives in writing the report
    C. select your statistical material
    D. obtain the necessary data from the files

20. Generally, the frequency with which reports are to be submitted or the length of the interval which they cover should depend MAINLY on the   20.___
    A. amount of time needed to prepare the reports
    B. degree of comprehensiveness required in the reports
    C. availability of the data to be included in the reports
    D. extent of the variations in the data with the passage of time

21. The objectiveness of a report is its unbiased presentation of the facts.   21.___
    If this be so, which of the following reports listed below is likely to be the MOST objective?
    A. The Best Use of an Electronic Computer in Department Z
    B. The Case for Raising the Salaries of Employees in Department A
    C. Quarterly Summary of Production in the Duplicating Unit of Department Y
    D. Recommendation to Terminate Employee X's Services Because of Misconduct

Questions 22-27.

DIRECTIONS: Questions 22 through 27 are to be answered SOLELY on
the basis of the information contained in the charts
below which relate to the budget allocations of City X,
a small suburban community. The charts depict the
annual budget allocations by Department and by Expenditures over a five-year period.

CITY X BUDGET IN MILLIONS OF DOLLARS

TABLE I. Budget Allocations By Department

Department	1997	1998	1999	2000	2001
Public Safety	30	45	50	40	50
Health and Welfare	50	75	90	60	70
Engineering	5	8	10	5	8
Human Resources	10	12	20	10	22
Conversation and Environment	10	15	20	20	15
Education and Development	15	25	35	15	15
TOTAL BUDGET	120	180	225	150	180

TABLE II. Budget Allocations By Expenditures

Category	1997	1998	1999	2000	2001
Raw Materials and Machinery	36	63	68	30	98
Capital Outlay	12	27	56	15	18
Personal Services	72	90	101	105	64
TOTAL BUDGET	120	180	225	150	180

22. The year in which the SMALLEST percentage of the total
annual budget was allocated to the Department of Education and Development is
A. 1997   B. 1998   C. 2000   D. 2001   22.____

23. Assume that, in 2000, the Department of Conservation and
Environment divided its annual budget into the three
categories of expenditures and in exactly the same pro-
portion as the budget shown in Table II for the year
2000.
The amount allocated for capital outlay in the Department
of Conservation and Environment's 2000 budget was MOST
NEARLY ____ million.
A. $2   B. $4   C. $6   D. $10   23.____

24. From the year 1998 to the year 2000, the sum of the   24.___
    annual budgets for the Departments of Public Safety and
    Engineering showed an overall ____ of ____ million.
       A. decline; $8   B. increase; $7
       C. decline; $15   D. increase; $22

25. The LARGEST dollar increase in departmental budget   25.___
    allocations from one year to the next was in
       A. Public Safety from 1997 to 1998
       B. Health and Welfare from 1997 to 1998
       C. Education and Development from 1999 to 2000
       D. Human Resources from 1999 to 2000

26. During the five-year period, the annual budget of the   26.___
    Department of Human Resources was GREATER than the
    annual budget for the Department of Conservation and
    Environment in ____ of the years.
       A. none   B. one   C. two   D. three

27. If the total City X budget increases at the same rate   27.___
    from 2001 to 2002 as it did from 2000 to 2001, the total
    City X budget for 2002 will be MOST NEARLY ____ million.
       A. $180   B. $200   C. $210   D. $215

Questions 28-34.

DIRECTIONS: Questions 28 through 34 are to be answered SOLELY on
               the basis of the information contained in the graph
               below which relates to the work of a public agency.

No. of
work units
completed

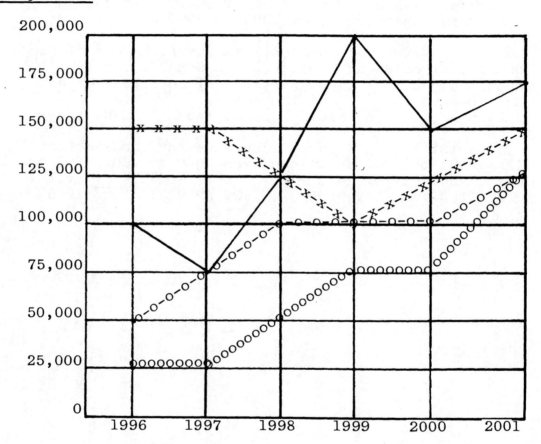

Units of each type of work completed by a public agency from
1996 to 2001.

Letters Written ─────────

Documents Filed ─x─x─x─x─x─x

Applications Processed ─o─o─o─o─o─o

Inspections made ooooooooooooo

28. The year for which the number of units of one type of   28.___
     work completed was LESS than it was for the previous
     year while the number of each of the other types of
     work completed was MORE than it was for the previous
     year was
         A. 1997   B. 1998   C. 1999   D. 2000

29. The number of letters written EXCEEDED the number of   29.___
     applications processed by the same amount in _____ of
     the years.
         A. two   B. three   C. four   D. five

30. The year in which the number of each type of work com-   30.___
     pleted was GREATER than in the preceding year was
         A. 1998   B. 1999   C. 2000   D. 2001

31. The number of applications processed and the number of   31.___
     documents filed were the SAME in
         A. 1997   B. 1998   C. 1999   D. 2000

32. The TOTAL number of units of work completed by the   32.___
     agency
         A. increased in each year after 1996
         B. decreased from the prior year in two of the years
            after 1996
         C. was the same in two successive years from 1996 to
            2001
         D. was less in 1996 than in any of the following years

33. For the year in which the number of letters written was   33.___
     twice as high as it was in 1996, the number of documents
     filed was _____ it was in 1996.
         A. the same as   B. two-thirds of what
         C. five-sixths of what   D. 1½ times what

34. The variable which was the MOST stable during the   34.___
     period 1996 through 2001 was
         A. Inspections Made   B. Letters Written
         C. Documents Filed   D. Applications Processed

Questions 35-41.

DIRECTIONS: Questions 35 through 41 are to be answered SOLELY on
              the basis of the information in the following passage.

     Job evaluation and job rating systems are intended to introduce
scientific procedures. Any type of approach, when properly used,
will give satisfactory results. The Point System, when properly
validated by actual use, is more likely to be suitable for general
use than the ranking system. In many aspects, the Factor Comparison
Plan is a point system tied to money values. Of course, there may
be another system that combines the ranking system with the point
system, especially during the initial stages of the development of
the program. After the program has been in use for some time, the
tendency is to drop off the ranking phase and continue the use of
the point system.

In the ranking system of rating of jobs, every job within the plant is arranged in some order, either from the one with the simplest qualifications to the one with maximum requirements, or in the reverse order. This system should be preceded by careful job analysis and the writing of accurate job descriptions before the rating process is undertaken. It is possible, of course, to take the jobs as they are found in the business enterprise and use the names as they are without any attempt at standardization, and merely rank them according to the general overall impression of the raters. Such a procedure is certain to fall short of what may reasonably be expected of job rating. Another procedure that is in reality merely a modification of the simple rating described above is to establish a series of grades or zones and arrange all the jobs in the plant into groups within these grades and zones. The practice in most common use is to arrange all the jobs in the plant according to their requirements by rating them and then to establish the classifications or groups.

The actual ranking of jobs may be done by one individual, several individuals, or a committee. If several individuals are working independently on the task, it will usually be found that, in general, they agree but that their rankings vary in certain details. A conference between the individuals, with each person giving his reasons why he rated one way or another, usually produces agreement. The detailed job descriptions are particularly helpful when there is disagreement among raters as to the rating of certain jobs. It is not only possible but desirable to have workers participate in the construction of the job description and in rating the job.

35. The MAIN theme of this passage is   35.____
    A. the elimination of bias in job rating
    B. the rating of jobs by the ranking system
    C. the need for accuracy in allocating points in the
       point system
    D. pitfalls to avoid in selecting key jobs in the Factor
       Comparison Plan

36. The ranking system of rating jobs consists MAINLY of   36.____
    A. attaching a point value to each ratable factor of
       each job prior to establishing an equitable pay
       scale
    B. arranging every job in the organization in descending
       order and then following this up with a job analysis
       of the key jobs
    C. preparing accurate job descriptions after a job ana-
       lysis and then arranging all jobs either in ascending
       or descending order based on job requirements
    D. arbitrarily establishing a hierarchy of job classes
       and grades and then fitting each job into a specific
       class and grade based on the opinions of unit super-
       visors

37. The above passage states that the system of classifying   37.___
    jobs MOST used in an organization is to
      A. organize all jobs in the organization in accordance
         with their requirements and then create categories
         or clusters of jobs
      B. classify all jobs in the organization according to
         the titles and rank by which they are currently
         known in the organization
      C. establish a pre-arranged series of grades or zones
         and then fit all jobs into one of the grades or zones
      D. determine the salary currently being paid for each
         job and then rank the jobs in order according to
         salary

38. According to the above passage, experience has shown   38.___
    that when a group of raters is assigned to the job
    evaluation task and each individual rates independently
    of the others, the raters GENERALLY
      A. agree with respect to all aspects of their rankings
      B. disagree with respect to all or nearly all aspects
         of the rankings
      C. disagree on overall ratings but agree on specific
         rating factors
      D. agree on overall rankings but have some variance
         in some details

39. The above passage states that the use of a detailed job   39.___
    description is of SPECIAL value when
      A. employees of an organization have participated in
         the preliminary steps involved in actual prepara-
         tion of the job description
      B. labor representatives are not participating in
         ranking of the jobs
      C. an individual rater who is unsure of himself is
         ranking the jobs
      D. a group of raters is having difficulty reaching
         unanimity with respect to ranking a certain job

40. A comparison of the various rating systems as described   40.___
    in the above passage shows that
      A. the ranking system is not as appropriate for general
         use as a properly validated point system
      B. the point system is the same as the Factor Comparison
         Plan except that it places greater emphasis on money
      C. no system is capable of combining the point system
         and the Factor Comparison Plan
      D. the point system will be discontinued last when
         used in combination with the Factor Comparison
         System

41. The above passage implies that the PRINCIPAL reason for
    creating job evaluation and rating systems was to help
    A. overcome union opposition to existing salary plans
    B. base wage determination on a more objective and
       orderly foundation
    C. eliminate personal bias on the part of the trained
       scientific job evaluators
    D. management determine if it was overpricing the
       various jobs in the organizational hierarchy

41.___

42. As a general rule, in a large office it is desirable to
    have more than one employee who is able to operate any
    one machine and more than one office machine capable of
    performing any one type of required operation.
    According to this statement, there USUALLY should be
    A. fewer office machines in an office than are necessary
       for efficient job performance
    B. more office machines in an office than there are
       employees able to operate them
    C. more types of required operations to be performed
       than there are machines necessary to their perfor-
       mance
    D. fewer types of required operations to be performed
       than there are machines capable of performing them

42.___

43. The plan of an organization's structure and procedures
    may appear to be perfectly sound, but the organization
    may still operate wastefully and with a great amount of
    friction because of the failure of the people in the
    organization to work together.
    The MOST valid implication of this statement is that
    A. inefficiency within an organization may be caused
       by people being directed to do the wrong things
    B. an organization which operates inefficiently might
       be improved by revising its systems and methods of
       operations
    C. use of the best methods an organization can devise
       may not prevent an organization from being ineffi-
       cient
    D. the people in an organization may not have an appre-
       ciation of the high quality of the organization's
       plan of operations

43.___

44. If an employee is to be held responsible for obtaining
    results, he should be given every reasonable freedom to
    exercise his own intelligence and initiative to achieve
    the results expected.
    The MOST valid implication of this statement is that
    A. the authority delegated should match the responsi-
       bility assigned
    B. achieving results depends upon the individual's
       willingness to work
    C. the most important aspect of getting a job done is
       to know how to do it
    D. understanding the requirements of a task is essen-
       tial to its accomplishment

44.___

45. Essentially, an organization is defined as any group of individuals who are cooperating under the direction of executive leadership in an attempt to accomplish certain common objectives.
The one of the following which this statement does NOT include as an essential characteristic of an organization is _____ the members of the group.
    A. cooperation among
    B. proficiency of
    C. authoritative guidance of
    D. goals common to

45.___

46. A supervisor, in organizing the work activities of the staff of an office, should recognize that one of the conditions which is expected to promote a high level of interest on the part of an office worker in his job is to assign him to perform a variety of work.
The MOST valid implication of this statement is that
    A. each worker should be taught to perform each type of work in the office
    B. workers should be assigned to perform types of work in which they have expressed interest
    C. a worker who is assigned to perform a single type of work is likely to become bored
    D. some workers are likely to perform several types of work better than other workers are able to

46.___

47. Of the following basic guides to effective letter writing, which one would NOT be recommended as a way of improving the quality of business letters?
    A. Use emphatic phrases like *close proximity* and *first and foremost* to round out sentences.
    B. Break up complicated sentences by making short sentences out of dependent clauses.
    C. Replace old-fashioned phrases like *enclosed please find* and *recent date* with a more direct approach.
    D. Personalize letters by using your reader's name at least once in the body of the message.

47.___

48. Suppose that you must write a reply letter to a citizen's request for a certain pamphlet printed by your agency. The pamphlet is temporarily unavailable but a new supply will be arriving by December 8 or 9.
Of the following four sentences, which one expresses the MOST positive business letter writing approach?
    A. We cannot send the materials you requested until after December 8.
    B. May we assure you that the materials you requested will be sent as quickly as possible.
    C. We will be sending the materials you requested as soon as our supply is replenished.
    D. We will mail the materials you requested on or shortly after December 8.

48.___

49. Using form letters in business correspondence is LEAST 49.___
effective when
    A. answering letters on a frequently recurring subject
    B. giving the same information to many addresses
    C. the recipient is only interested in the routine
       information contained in the form letter
    D. a reply must be keyed to the individual require-
       ments of the intended reader

50. The ability to write memos and letters is very important 50.___
in clerical and administrative work. Methodical planning
of a reply letter usually involves the following basic
steps which are arranged in random order:
    I. Determine the purpose of the letter you are about
      to write.
   II. Make an outline of what information your reply
      letter should contain.
  III. Read carefully the letter to be answered to find
      out its main points.
   IV. Assemble the facts to be included in your reply
      letter.
    V. Visualize your intended reader and adapt your letter
      writing style to him.

If the above-numbered steps were arranged in their proper
logical order, the one which would be THIRD in the
sequence is
    A. II   B. III   C. IV   D. V

KEY (CORRECT ANSWERS)

1. A	11. C	21. C	31. C	41. B
2. B	12. C	22. D	32. C	42. D
3. C	13. A	23. A	33. B	43. C
4. C	14. B	24. A	34. D	44. A
5. B	15. C	25. B	35. B	45. B
6. C	16. D	26. B	36. C	46. C
7. D	17. B	27. D	37. A	47. A
8. D	18. A	28. B	38. D	48. D
9. B	19. B	29. B	39. D	49. D
10. A	20. D	30. D	40. A	50. A

EXAMINATION SECTION

TEST 1

DIRECTIONS: Each question or incomplete statement is followed by several suggested answers or completions. Select the one that BEST answers the question or completes the statement. *PRINT THE LETTER OF THE CORRECT ANSWER IN THE SPACE AT THE RIGHT.*

Questions 1-4.

DIRECTIONS: Answer Questions 1 through 4 SOLELY on the basis of the following passage.

Job analysis combined with performance appraisal is an excellent method of determining training needs of individuals. The steps in this method are to determine the specific duties of the job, to evaluate the adequacy with which the employee performs each of these duties, and finally to determine what significant improvements can be made by training.

The list of duties can be obtained in a number of ways: asking the employee, asking the supervisor, observing the employee, etc. Adequacy of performance can be estimated by the employee, but the supervisor's evaluation must also be obtained. This evaluation will usually be based on observation.

What does the supervisor observe? The employee, while he is working; the employee's work relationships; the ease, speed, and sureness of the employee's actions; the way he applies himself to the job; the accuracy and amount of completed work; its conformity with established procedures and standards; the appearance of the work; the soundness of judgment it shows; and, finally, signs of good or poor communication, understanding, and cooperation among employees.

Such observation is a normal and inseparable part of the every-day job of supervision. Systematically recorded, evaluated, and summarized, it highlights both general and individual training needs.

1. According to the passage, job analysis may be used by the supervisor in   1.___
   A. increasing his own understanding of tasks performed in his unit
   B. increasing efficiency of communication within the organization
   C. assisting personnel experts in the classification of positions
   D. determining in which areas an employee needs more instruction

2. According to the passage, the FIRST step in determining
    the training needs of employees is to
    A. locate the significant improvements that can be
       made by training
    B. determine the specific duties required in a job
    C. evaluate the employee's performance
    D. motivate the employee to want to improve himself

2.___

3. On the basis of the above passage, which of the following
    is the BEST way for a supervisor to determine the adequacy
    of employee performance?
    A. Check the accuracy and amount of completed work
    B. Ask the training officer
    C. Observe all aspects of the employee's work
    D. Obtain the employee's own estimate

3.___

4. Which of the following is NOT mentioned by the passage as
    a factor to be taken into consideration in judging the
    adequacy of employee performance?
    A. Accuracy of completed work
    B. Appearance of completed work
    C. Cooperation among employees
    D. Attitude of the employee toward his supervisor

4.___

5. In indexing names of business firms and other organizations,
    ONE of the rules to be followed is:
    A. The word *and* is considered an indexing unit
    B. When a firm name includes the full name of a person
       who is not well-known, the person's first name is
       considered as the first indexing unit
    C. Usually the units in a firm name are indexed in the
       order in which they are written
    D. When a firm's name is made up of single letters (such
       as ABC Corp.), the letters taken together are con-
       sidered more than one indexing unit

5.___

6. Assume that people often come to your office with com-
    plaints of errors in your agency's handling of their
    clients. The employees in your office have the job of
    listening to these complaints and investigating them.
    One day, when it is almost closing time, a person comes
    into your office, apparently very angry, and demands that
    you take care of his complaint at once.
    Your IMMEDIATE reaction should be to
    A. suggest that he return the following day
    B. find out his name and the nature of his complaint
    C. tell him to write a letter
    D. call over your superior

6.___

7. Assume that part of your job is to notify people concerning
    whether their applications for a certain program have been
    approved or disapproved. However, you do not actually make
    the decision on approval or disapproval. One day, you
    answer a telephone call from a woman who states that she
    has not yet received any word on her application. She goes
    on to tell you her qualifications for the program. From
    what she has said, you know that persons with such qualifi-
    cations are usually approved.

7.___

Of the following, which one is the BEST thing for you to say to her?
   A. "You probably will be accepted, but wait until you receive a letter before trying to join the program."
   B. "Since you seem well qualified, I am sure that your application will be approved."
   C. "If you can write us a letter emphasizing your qualifications, it may speed up the process."
   D. "You will be notified of the results of your application as soon as a decision has been made."

8. Suppose that one of your duties includes answering specific telephone inquiries. Your superior refers a call to you from an irate person who claims that your agency is inefficient and is wasting taxpayers' money.
Of the following, the BEST way to handle such a call is to
   A. listen briefly and then hang up without answering
   B. note the caller's comments and tell him that you will transmit them to your superiors
   C. connect the caller with the head of your agency
   D. discuss your own opinions with the caller

8.___

9. An employee has been assigned to open her division head's mail and place it on his desk. One day, the employee opens a letter which she then notices is marked *Personal*.
Of the following, the BEST action for her to take is to
   A. write *Personal* on the letter and staple the envelope to the back of the letter
   B. ignore the matter and treat the letter the same way as the others
   C. give it to another division head to hold until her own division head comes into the office
   D. leave the letter in the envelope and write *Sorry - opened by mistake* on the envelope and initial it

9.___

Questions 10-14.

DIRECTIONS: Questions 10 through 14 each consist of a quotation which contains one word that is incorrectly used because it is not in keeping with the meaning that the quotation is evidently intended to convey. Of the words underlined in each quotation, determine which word is incorrectly used. Then select from among the words lettered A, B, C, and D the word which, when substituted for the incorrectly used word, would BEST help to convey the meaning of the quotation. (Do NOT indicate a change for an underlined word unless the underlined word is incorrectly used.)

10. Unless reasonable managerial supervision is exercised over office supplies, it is certain that there will be extravagance, rejected items out of stock, excessive prices paid for certain items, and obsolete material in the stockroom.
   A. overlooked   B. immoderate
   C. needed   D. instituted

10.___

11. Since office supplies are in such common use, an
    attitude of indifference about their handling is not
    unusual. Their importance is often recognized only when
    they are utilized or out of stock, for office employees
    must have proper supplies if maximum productivity is to
    be attained.
    A. plentiful   B. unavailable
    C. reduced   D. expected

11.___

12. Anyone effected by paperwork, interested in or engaged in
    office work, or desiring to improve informational
    activities can find materials keyed to his needs.
    A. attentive   B. available   C. affected   D. ambitious

12.___

13. Information is homogeneous and must therefore be properly
    classified so that each type may be employed in ways
    appropriate to its own peculiar properties.
    A. apparent   B. heterogeneous
    C. consistent   D. idiosyncratic

13.___

14. Intellectual training may seem a formidable phrase, but
    it means nothing more than the deliberate cultivation of
    the ability to think, and there is no dark contrast between
    the intellectual and the practical.
    A. subjective   B. objective
    C. sharp   D. vocational

14.___

15. The MOST important reason for having a filing system is
    to
    A. get papers out of the way
    B. have a record of everything that has happened
    C. retain information to justify your actions
    D. enable rapid retrieval of information

15.___

16. The system of filing which is used MOST frequently is
    called ____ filing.
    A. alphabetic   B. alphanumeric
    C. geographic   D. numeric

16.___

17. One of the clerks under your supervision has been tele-
    phoning frequently to tell you that he was taking the day
    off. Unless there is a real need for it, taking leave
    which is not scheduled is frowned upon because it upsets
    the work schedule.
    Under these circumstances, which of the following reasons
    for taking the day off is MOST acceptable?
    A. "I can't work when my arthritis bothers me."
    B. "I've been pressured with work from my night job and
        needed the extra time to catch up."
    C. "My family just moved to a new house, and I needed the
        time to start the repairs."
    D. "Work here has not been challenging, and I've been
        looking for another job."

17.___

18. One of the employees under your supervision, previously   18.____
a very satisfactory worker, has begun arriving late one
or two mornings each week. No explanation has been
offered for this change. You call her to your office for
a conference. As you are explaining the purpose of the
conference and your need to understand this sudden lateness
problem, she becomes angry and states that you have no
right to question her.
Of the following, the BEST course of action for you to take
at this point is to
    A. inform her in your most authoritarian tone that you are
       the supervisor and that you have every right to
       question her
    B. end the conference and advise the employee that you
       will have no further discussion with her until she
       controls her temper
    C. remain calm, try to calm her down, and when she has
       quieted, explain the reasons for your questions and
       the need for answers
    D. hold your temper; when she has calmed down, tell her
       that you will not have a tardy worker in your unit
       and will have her transferred at once

19. Assume that, in the branch of the agency for which you   19.____
work, you are the only clerical person on the staff with
a supervisory title and, in addition, that you are the
office manager. On a particular day when all members of
the professional staff are away from the building attending
an important meeting, an urgent call comes through re-
questing some confidential information ordinarily released
only by professional staff.
Of the following, the MOST reasonable action for you to
take is to
    A. decline to give the information because you are not
       a member of the professional staff
    B. offer to call back after you get permission from the
       agency director at the main office
    C. advise the caller that you will supply the information
       as soon as your chief returns
    D. supply the information requested and inform your
       chief when she returns

20. As a supervisor, you are scheduled to attend an important   20.____
conference with your superior. However, that day you
learn that your very capable assistant is ill and unable
to come to work. Several highly sensitive tasks are
scheduled for completion on this day.
Of the following, the BEST way to handle this situation
is to
    A. tell your supervisor you cannot attend the meeting
       and ask that it be postponed
    B. assign one of your staff to see that the jobs are
       completed and turned in
    C. advise your supervisor of the situation and ask
       what you should do
    D. call the departments for which the work is being
       done and ask for an extension of time

21. When a decision needs to be made which is likely to   21._____
    affect units other than his own, a supervisor should
    USUALLY
    A. make such a decision quickly and then discuss it
       with his supervisor
    B. make such a decision only after careful consultation
       with his subordinates
    C. discuss the problem with his immediate superior
       before making such a decision
    D. have his subordinates arrive at such a decision in
       conference with the subordinates in the other units

22. Assume that, as a supervisor in Division X, you are   22._____
    training Ms. Y, a new employee, to answer the telephone
    properly.
    You should explain that the BEST way to answer is to pick
    up the receiver and say:
    A. "What is your name, please?"
    B. "May I help you?"
    C. "Ms. Y speaking."
    D. "Division X, Ms. Y speaking."

Questions 23-25.

DIRECTIONS: Questions 23 through 25 consist of sentences in which
              two words are missing. Examine each sentence, and
              then choose from below it the words which should be
              inserted in the blank spaces in order to create a
              coherent and well-written sentence.

23. Human behavior is far ____ variable, and therefore ____   23._____
    predictable, than that of any other species.
    A. less; as   B. less; not
    C. more; not   D. more; less

24. The ____ limitation of this method is that the results   24._____
    are based ____ a narrow sample.
    A. chief; with   B. chief; on
    C. only; for   D. only; to

25. Although there ____ a standard procedure for handling   25._____
    these problems, each case often has ____ own unique
    features.
    A. are; its   B. are; their
    C. is; its   D. is; their

KEY (CORRECT ANSWERS)

1. D	6. B	11. B	16. A	21. C
2. B	7. D	12. C	17. A	22. D
3. C	8. B	13. B	18. C	23. D
4. D	9. D	14. C	19. B	24. B
5. C	10. C	15. D	20. C	25. C

TEST 2

DIRECTIONS: Each question or incomplete statement is followed by several suggested answers or completions. Select the one that BEST answers your question or completes the statement. *PRINT THE LETTER OF THE CORRECT ANSWER IN THE SPACE AT THE RIGHT.*

Questions 1-3.

DIRECTIONS: Questions 1 through 3 each consist of a group of four sentences. Read each sentence carefully, and select the one of the four in each group which represents the BEST English usage for business letters and reports.

1. A. The chairman himself, rather than his aides, has reviewed the report.
   B. The chairman himself, rather than his aides, have reviewed the report.
   C. The chairmen, not the aide, has reviewed the report.
   D. The aide, not the chairmen, have reviewed the report.

   1.___

2. A. Various proposals were submitted but the decision is not been made.
   B. Various proposals has been submitted but the decision has not been made.
   C. Various proposals were submitted but the decision is not been made.
   D. Various proposals have been submitted but the decision has not been made.

   2.___

3. A. Everyone were rewarded for his successful attempt.
   B. They were successful in their attempts and each of them was rewarded.
   C. Each of them are rewarded for their successful attempts.
   D. The reward for their successful attempts were made to each of them.

   3.___

4. Which of the following is MOST suited to arrangement in chronological order?
   A. Applications for various types and levels of jobs
   B. Issues of a weekly publication
   C. Weekly time cards for all employees for the week of April 21
   D. Personnel records for all employees

   4.___

5. Words that are *synonymous* with a given word ALWAYS
   A. have the same meaning as the given word
   B. have the same pronunciation as the given word
   C. have the opposite meaning of the given word
   D. can be rhymed with the given word

   5.___

Questions 6-11.

DIRECTIONS: Answer Questions 6 through 11 on the basis of the following chart showing numbers of errors made by four clerks in one work unit for a half-year period.

	Allan	Barry	Cary	David
July	5	4	1	7
Aug.	8	3	9	8
Sept.	7	8	7	5
Oct.	3	6	5	3
Nov.	2	4	4	6
Dec.	5	2	8	4

6. The clerk with the HIGHEST number of errors for the six-month period was
   A. Allan   B. Barry   C. Cary   D. David   6.____

7. If the number of errors made by Allan in the six months shown represented one-eighth of the total errors made by the unit during the entire year, what was the TOTAL number of errors made by the unit for the year?
   A. 124   B. 180   C. 240   D. 360   7.____

8. The number of errors made by David in November was what FRACTION of the total errors made in November?
   A. 1/3   B. 1/6   C. 3/8   D. 3/16   8.____

9. The average number of errors made per month per clerk was MOST NEARLY
   A. 4   B. 5   C. 6   D. 7   9.____

10. Of the total number of errors made during the six-month period, the percentage made in August was MOST NEARLY
    A. 2%   B. 4%   C. 23%   D. 44%   10.____

11. If the number of errors in the unit were to decrease in the next six months by 30%, what would be MOST NEARLY the total number of errors for the unit for the next six months?
    A. 87   B. 94   C. 120   D. 137   11.____

12. The arithmetic mean salary for five employees earning $18,500, $18,300, $18,600, $18,400, and $18,500, respectively, is
    A. $18,450   B. $18,460   C. $18,475   D. $18,500   12.____

13. Last year, a city department which is responsible for   13.___
    purchasing supplies ordered bond paper in equal quantities
    from 22 different companies. The price was exactly the
    same for each company, and the total cost for the 22
    orders was $693,113.
    Assuming prices did not change during the year, the cost
    of EACH order was MOST NEARLY
       A. $31,490   B. $31,495   C. $31,500   D. $31,505

14. A city agency engaged in repair work uses a small part   14.___
    which the city purchases for 14¢ each. Assume that, in
    a certain year, the total expenditure of the city for
    this part was $700.
    How MANY of these parts were purchased that year?
       A. 50   B. 200   C. 2,000   D. 5,000

15. The work unit which you supervise is responsible for   15.___
    processing fifteen reports per month.
    If your unit has four clerks and the best worker completes
    40% of the reports himself, how many reports would each
    of the other clerks have to complete if they all do an
    equal number?
       A. 1   B. 2   C. 3   D. 4

16. Assume that the work unit in which you work has 24 clerks   16.___
    and 18 stenographers.
    In order to change the ratio of stenographers to clerks
    so that there is one stenographer for every four clerks,
    it would be necessary to REDUCE the number of stenographers
    by
       A. 3   B. 6   C. 9   D. 12

17. Assume that your office is responsible for opening and   17.___
    distributing all the mail of the division. After opening
    a letter, one of your subordinates notices that it states
    that there should be an enclosure in the envelope. However,
    there is no enclosure in the envelope.
    Of the following, the BEST instruction that you can give
    the clerk is to
       A. call the sender to obtain the enclosure
       B. call the addressee to inform him that the enclosure
          is missing
       C. note the omission in the margin of the letter
       D. forward the letter without taking any action

18. While opening the envelope containing official correspon-   18.___
    dence, you accidentally cut the enclosed letter.
    Of the following, the BEST action for you to take is to
       A. leave the material as it is
       B. put it together by using transparent mending tape
       C. keep it together by putting it back in the envelope
       D. keep it together by using paper clips

19. Suppose your supervisor is on the telephone in his office   19. ___
and an applicant arrives for a scheduled interview with
him.
Of the following, the BEST procedure to follow ordinarily
is to
   A. informally chat with the applicant in your office
      until your supervisor has finished his phone
      conversation
   B. escort him directly into your supervisor's office
      and have him wait for him there
   C. inform your supervisor of the applicant's arrival
      and try to make the applicant feel comfortable while
      waiting
   D. have him hang up his coat and tell him to go directly
      in to see your supervisor

20. The length of time that files should be kept is GENERALLY   20. ___
   A. considered to be seven years
   B. dependent upon how much new material has accumulated
      in the files
   C. directly proportionate to the number of years the
      office has been in operation
   D. dependent upon the type and nature of the material
      in the files

21. Cross-referencing a document when you file it means   21. ___
   A. making a copy of the document and putting the copy
      into a related file
   B. indicating on the front of the document the name of
      the person who wrote it, the date it was written,
      and for what purpose
   C. putting a special sheet or card in a related file to
      indicate where the document is filed
   D. indicating on the document where it is to be filed

22. Unnecessary handling and recording of incoming mail could   22. ___
be eliminated by
   A. having the person who opens it initial it
   B. indicating on the piece of mail the names of all the
      individuals who should see it
   C. sending all incoming mail to more than one central
      location
   D. making a photocopy of each piece of incoming mail

23. Of the following, the office tasks which lend themselves   23. ___
MOST readily to planning and study are
   A. repetitive, occur in volume, and extend over a
      period of time
   B. cyclical in nature, have small volume, and extend
      over a short period of time
   C. tasks which occur only once in a great while not
      according to any schedule, and have large volume
   D. special tasks which occur only once, regardless of
      their volume and length of time

24. A good recordkeeping system includes all of the following   24.____
    procedures EXCEPT the
    A. filing of useless records
    B. destruction of certain files
    C. transferring of records from one type of file to
       another
    D. creation of inactive files

25. Assume that, as a supervisor, you are responsible for   25.____
    orienting and training new employees in your unit.
    Which of the following can MOST properly be omitted from
    your discussions with a new employee?
    A. The purpose of commonly used office forms
    B. Time and leave regulations
    C. Procedures for required handling of routine business
       calls
    D. The reason the last employee was fired

KEY (CORRECT ANSWERS)

1.	A	11.	A
2.	D	12.	B
3.	B	13.	D
4.	B	14.	D
5.	A	15.	C
6.	C	16.	D
7.	C	17.	C
8.	C	18.	B
9.	B	19.	C
10.	C	20.	D

21.	C
22.	B
23.	A
24.	A
25.	D

READING COMPREHENSION
UNDERSTANDING AND INTERPRETING WRITTEN MATERIAL
EXAMINATION SECTION

DIRECTIONS: Each question or incomplete statement is followed by several suggested answers or completions. Select the one that BEST answers the question or completes the statement. *PRINT THE LETTER OF THE CORRECT ANSWER IN THE SPACE AT THE RIGHT.*

TEST 1

Questions 1-5.

DIRECTIONS: Questions 1 through 5 are to be answered SOLELY on the basis of the following passage.

The most effective control mechanism to prevent gross incompetence on the part of public employees is a good personnel program. The personnel officer in the line departments and the central personnel agency should exert positive leadership to raise levels of performance. Although the key factor is the quality of the personnel recruited, staff members other than personnel officers can make important contributions to efficiency. Administrative analysts, now employed in many agencies, make detailed studies of organization and procedures, with the purpose of eliminating delays, waste, and other inefficiencies. Efficiency is, however, more than a question of good organization and procedures; it is also the product of the attitudes and values of the public employees. Personal motivation can provide the will to be efficient. The best management studies will not result in substantial improvement of the performance of those employees who feel no great urge to work up to their abilities.

1. The above passage indicates that the KEY factor in prevent-   1.___
    ing gross incompetence of public employees is the
    A. hiring of administrative analysts to assist personnel
       people
    B. utilization of effective management studies
    C. overlapping of responsibility
    D. quality of the employees hired

2. According to the above passage, the central personnel   2.___
    agency staff SHOULD
    A. work more closely with administrative analysts in
       the line departments than with personnel officers
    B. make a serious effort to avoid jurisdictional con-
       flicts with personnel officers in line departments
    C. contribute to improving the quality of work of
       public employees
    D. engage in a comprehensive program to change the
       public's negative image of public employees

3. The above passage indicates that efficiency in an organi-   3.___
    zation can BEST be brought about by
    A. eliminating ineffective control mechanisms

      B. instituting sound organizational procedures
      C. promoting competent personnel
      D. recruiting people with desire to do good work

4. According to the above passage, the purpose of administra-   4.___
   tive analysis in a public agency is to
      A. prevent injustice to the public employee
      B. promote the efficiency of the agency
      C. protect the interests of the public
      D. ensure the observance of procedural due process

5. The above passage implies that a considerable rise in the   5.___
   quality of work of public employees can be brought about by
      A. encouraging positive employee attitudes toward work
      B. controlling personnel officers who exceed their powers
      C. creating warm personal associations among public
         employees in an agency
      D. closing loopholes in personnel organization and
         procedures

Questions 6-8.

DIRECTIONS: Questions 6 through 8 are to be answered SOLELY on
             the basis of the following passage on Employee Needs.

EMPLOYEE NEEDS

The greatest waste in industry and in government may be that of
human resources. This waste usually derives not from employees'
unwillingness or inability, but from management's ineptness to meet
the maintenance and motivational needs of employees. Maintenance
needs refer to such needs as providing employees with safe places to
work, written work rules, job security, adequate salary, employer-
sponsored social activities, and with knowledge of their role in the
overall framework of the organization. However, of greatest signifi-
cance to employees are the motivational needs of job growth, achievement, responsibility, and recognition.

Although employee dissatisfaction may stem from either poor
maintenance or poor motivation factors, the outward manifestation of
the dissatisfaction may be very much alike, i.e., negativism, complaints, deterioration of performance, and so forth. The improvement
in the lighting of an employee's work area or raising his level of
pay won't do much good if the source of the dissatisfaction is the
absence of a meaningful assignment. By the same token, if an employee
is dissatisfied with what he considers inequitable pay, the introduction of additional challenge in his work may simply make matters worse.

It is relatively easy for an employee to express frustration by
complaining about pay, washroom conditions, fringe benefits, and so
forth; but most people cannot easily express resentment in terms of
the more abstract concepts concerning job growth, responsibility,
and achievement.

It would be wrong to assume that there is no interaction between maintenance and motivational needs of employees. For example, conditions of high motivation often overshadow poor maintenance conditions. If an organization is in a period of strong growth and expansion, opportunities for job growth, responsibility, recognition, and achievement are usually abundant, but the rapid growth may have outrun the upkeep of maintenance factors. In this situation, motivation may be high, but only if employees recognize the poor maintenance conditions as unavoidable and temporary. The subordination of maintenance factors cannot go on indefinitely, even with the highest motivation.

Both maintenance and motivation factors influence the behavior of all employees, but employees are not identical and, furthermore, the needs of any individual do not remain constant. However, a broad distinction can be made between employees who have a basic orientation toward maintenance factors and those with greater sensitivity toward motivation factors.

A highly maintenance-oriented individual, preoccupied with the factors peripheral to his job rather than the job itself, is more concerned with comfort than challenge. He does not get deeply involved with his work but does with the condition of his work area, toilet facilities, and his time for going to lunch. By contrast, a strongly motivation-oriented employee is usually relatively indifferent to his surroundings and is caught up in the pursuit of work goals.

Fortunately, there are few people who are either exclusively maintenance-oriented or purely motivation-oriented. The former would be deadwood in an organization, while the latter might trample on those around him in his pursuit to achieve his goals.

6. With respect to employee motivational and maintenance   6.___
    needs, the management policies of an organization which
    is growing rapidly will PROBABLY result
    A. more in meeting motivational needs rather than
       maintenance needs
    B. more in meeting maintenance needs rather than
       motivational needs
    C. in meeting both of these needs equally
    D. in increased effort to define the motivational and
       maintenance needs of its employees

7. In accordance with the above passage, which of the follow-   7.___
    ing CANNOT be considered as an example of an employee
    maintenance need for railroad clerks?
    A. Providing more relief periods
    B. Providing fair salary increases at periodic intervals
    C. Increasing job responsibilities
    D. Increasing health insurance benefits

8. Most employees in an organization may be categorized as   8.___
    being interested in
    A. maintenance needs *only*
    B. motivational needs *only*
    C. both motivational and maintenance needs
    D. money only, to the exclusion of all other needs

Questions 9-11.

DIRECTIONS: Questions 9 through 11 are to be answered SOLELY on
the basis of the following passage on Good Employee
Practices.

GOOD EMPLOYEE PRACTICES

As a city employee, you will be expected to take an interest in
your work and perform the duties of your job to the best of your
ability and in a spirit of cooperation. Nothing shows an interest in
your work more than coming to work on time, not only at the start of
the day but also when returning from lunch. If it is necessary for
you to keep a personal appointment at lunch hour which might cause a
delay in getting back to work on time, you should explain the situation to your supervisor and get his approval to come back a little
late before you leave for lunch.

You should do everything that is asked of you willingly and
consider important even the small jobs that your supervisor gives you.
Although these jobs may seem unimportant, if you forget to do them or
if you don't do them right, trouble may develop later.

Getting along well with your fellow workers will add much to the
enjoyment of your work. You should respect your fellow workers and
try to see their side when a disagreement arises. The better you
get along with your fellow workers and your supervisor, the better you
will like your job and the better you will be able to do it.

9.   According to the above passage, in your job as a city   9.___
     employee, you are expected to
        A. show a willingness to cooperate on the job
        B. get your supervisor's approval before keeping any
           personal appointments at lunch hour
        C. avoid doing small jobs that seem unimportant
        D. do the easier jobs at the start of the day and the
           more difficult ones later on

10. According to the above passage, getting to work on time   10.___
     shows that you
        A. need the job
        B. have an interest in your work
        C. get along well with your fellow workers
        D. like your supervisor

11. According to the above passage, the one of the following   11.___
     statements that is NOT true is
        A. if you do a small job wrong, trouble may develop
        B. you should respect your fellow workers
        C. if you disagree with a fellow worker, you should try
           to see his side of the story
        D. the less you get along with your supervisor, the
           better you will be able to do your job

Questions 12-15.

DIRECTIONS: Questions 12 through 15 are to be answered SOLELY on
the basis of the following passage on Employee Suggestions.

EMPLOYEE SUGGESTIONS

To increase the effectiveness of the city government, the city
asks its employees to offer suggestions when they feel an improvement
could be made in some government operation. The Employees' Suggestions
Program was started to encourage city employees to do this. Through
this Program, which is only for city employees, cash awards may be
given to those whose suggestions are submitted and approved. Suggestions are looked for not only from supervisors but from all city
employees as any city employee may get an idea which might be approved
and contribute greatly to the solution of some problem of city government.

Therefore, all suggestions for improvement are welcome, whether
they be suggestions on how to improve working conditions, or on how
to increase the speed with which work is done, or on how to reduce or
eliminate such things as waste, time losses, accidents or fire hazards.
There are, however, a few types of suggestions for which cash awards
cannot be given. An example of this type would be a suggestion to
increase salaries or a suggestion to change the regulations about
annual leave or about sick leave. The number of suggestions sent in
has increased sharply during the past few years. It is hoped that it
will keep increasing in the future in order to meet the city's needs
for more ideas for improved ways of doing things.

12. According to the above passage, the MAIN reason why the   12.____
    city asks its employees for suggestions about government
    operations is to
        A. increase the effectiveness of the city government
        B. show that the Employees' Suggestion Program is working
           well
        C. show that everybody helps run the city government
        D. have the employee win a prize

13. According to the above passage, the Employees' Suggestion   13.____
    Program can approve awards ONLY for those suggestions that
    come from
        A. city employees
        B. city employees who are supervisors
        C. city employees who are not supervisors
        D. experienced employees of the city

14. According to the above passage, a cash award cannot be   14.____
    given through the Employees' Suggestion Program for a
    suggestion about
        A. getting work done faster
        B. helping prevent accidents on the job
        C. increasing the amount of annual leave for city employees
        D. reducing the chance of fire where city employees work

5

15. According to the above passage, the suggestions sent in 15.____
during the past few years have
  A. all been approved
  B. generally been well written
  C. been mostly about reducing or eliminating waste
  D. been greater in number than before

Questions 16-18.

DIRECTIONS: Questions 16 through 18 are to be answered SOLELY on
the basis of the following passage.

The supervisor will gain the respect of the members of his staff
and increase his influence over them by controlling his temper and
avoiding criticizing anyone publicly. When a mistake is made, the
good supervisor will talk it over with the employee quietly and privately. The supervisor will listen to the employee's story, suggest
the better way of doing the job, and offer help so the mistake won't
happen again. Before closing the discussion, the supervisor should
try to find something good to say about other parts of the employee's
work. Some praise and appreciation, along with instruction, is more
likely to encourage an employee to improve in those areas where he
is weakest.

16. A GOOD title that would show the meaning of the above 16.____
passage would be
  A. HOW TO CORRECT EMPLOYEE ERRORS
  B. HOW TO PRAISE EMPLOYEES
  C. MISTAKES ARE PREVENTABLE
  D. THE WEAK EMPLOYEE

17. According to the above passage, the work of an employee 17.____
who has made a mistake is more likely to improve if the
supervisor
  A. avoids criticizing him
  B. gives him a chance to suggest a better way of doing
the work
  C. listens to the employee's excuses to see if he is right
  D. praises good work at the same time he corrects the
mistake

18. According to the above passage, when a supervisor needs 18.____
to correct an employee's mistake, it is important that he
  A. allow some time to go by after the mistake is made
  B. do so when other employees are not present
  C. show his influence with his tone of voice
  D. tell other employees to avoid the same mistake

Questions 19-23.

DIRECTIONS: Questions 19 through 23 are to be answered SOLELY on
the basis of the following passage.

In studying the relationships of people to the organizational
structure, it is absolutely necessary to identify and recognize the
informal organizational structure. These relationships are necessary

6

when coordination of a plan is attempted. They may be with *the boss,* line supervisors, staff personnel, or other representatives of the formal organization's hierarchy, and they may include the *liaison men* who serve as the leaders of the informal organization. An acquaintanceship with the people serving in these roles in the organization, and its formal counterpart, permits a supervisor to recognize sensitive areas in which it is simple to get a conflict reaction. Avoidance of such areas, plus conscious efforts to inform other people of his own objectives for various plans, will usually enlist their aid and support. Planning *without people* can lead to disaster because the individuals who must act together to make any plan a success are more important than the plans themselves.

19. Of the following titles, the one that MOST clearly describes the above passage is
    A. COORDINATION OF A FUNCTION
    B. AVOIDANCE OF CONFLICT
    C. PLANNING WITH PEOPLE
    D. PLANNING OBJECTIVES

19.____

20. According to the above passage, attempts at coordinating plans may fail unless
    A. the plan's objectives are clearly set forth
    B. conflict between groups is resolved
    C. the plans themselves are worthwhile
    D. informal relationships are recognized

20.____

21. According to the above passage, conflict
    A. may, in some cases, be desirable to secure results
    B. produces more heat than light
    C. should be avoided at all costs
    D. possibilities can be predicted by a sensitive supervisor

21.____

22. The above passage implies that
    A. informal relationships are more important than formal structure
    B. the weakness of a formal structure depends upon informal relationships
    C. liaison men are the key people to consult when taking formal and informal structures into account
    D. individuals in a group are at least as important as the plans for the group

22.____

23. The above passage suggests that
    A. some planning can be disastrous
    B. certain people in sensitive areas should be avoided
    C. the supervisor should discourage acquaintanceships in the organization
    D. organizational relationships should be consciously limited

23.____

Questions 24-25.

DIRECTIONS: Questions 24 and 25 are to be answered SOLELY on the basis of the following passage.

Good personnel relations of an organization depend upon mutual confidence, trust, and good will. The basis of confidence is understanding. Most troubles start with people who do not understand each other. When the organization's intentions or motives are misunderstood, or when reasons for actions, practices, or policies are misconstrued, complete cooperation from individuals is not forthcoming. If management expects full cooperation from employees, it has a responsibility of sharing with them the information which is the foundation of proper understanding, confidence, and trust. Personnel management has long since outgrown the days when it was the vogue to *treat them rough and tell them nothing*. Up-to-date personnel management provides all possible information about the activities, aims, and purposes of the organization. It seems altogether creditable that a desire should exist among employees for such information which the best-intentioned executive might think would not interest them and which the worst-intentioned would think was none of their business.

24.   The above passage implies that one of the causes of the   24.___
      difficulty which an organization might have with its
      personnel relations is that its employees
         A. have not expressed interest in the activities, aims,
            and purposes of the organization
         B. do not believe in the good faith of the organization
         C. have not been able to give full cooperation to the
            organization
         D. do not recommend improvements in the practices and
            policies of the organization

25.   According to the above passage, in order for an organiza-   25.___
      tion to have good personnel relations, it is NOT essential
      that
         A. employees have confidence in the organization
         B. the purposes of the organization be understood by
            the employees
         C. employees have a desire for information about the
            organization
         D. information about the organization be communicated
            to employees

TEST 2

Questions 1-8.

DIRECTIONS: Questions 1 through 8 are to be answered SOLELY on the basis of the following passage.

Important figures in education and in public affairs have recommended development of a private organization sponsored in part by various private foundations which would offer installment payment plans to full-time matriculated students in accredited colleges and universities in the United States and Canada. Contracts would be drawn to cover either tuition and fees, or tuition, fees, room and board in college facilities, from one year up to and including six years. A special charge, which would vary with the length of the contract, would be added to the gross repayable amount. This would be in addition to interest at a rate which would vary with the income of the parents. There would be a 3% annual interest charge for families with total income, before income taxes, of $10,000 or less. The rate would increase by 1/10 of 1% for every $200 of additional net income in excess of $10,000 up to a maximum of 10% interest. Contracts would carry an insurance provision on the life of the parent or guardian who signs the contract; all contracts must have the signature of a parent or guardian. Payment would be scheduled in equal monthly installments.

1. Which of the following students would be eligible for the payment plan described in the above passage? 1.___
   A
   A. matriculated student taking six semester hours toward a graduate degree
   B. matriculated student taking seventeen semester hours toward an undergraduate degree
   C. graduate matriculated at the University of Mexico taking eighteen semester hours toward a graduate degree
   D. student taking eighteen semester hours in a special pre-matriculation program

2. According to the above passage, the organization described would be sponsored in part by 2.___
   A. private foundations
   B. colleges and universities
   C. persons in the field of education
   D. persons in public life

3. Which of the following expenses could NOT be covered by a contract with the organization described in the above passage? 3.___
   A. Tuition amounting to $4,000 per year
   B. Registration and laboratory fees
   C. Meals at restaurants near the college
   D. Rent for an apartment in a college dormitory

4. The total amount to be paid would include ONLY the   4.___
     A. principal
     B. principal and interest
     C. principal, interest, and special charge
     D. principal, interest, special charge, and fee

5. The contract would carry insurance on the   5.___
     A. life of the student
     B. life of the student's parents
     C. income of the parents of the student
     D. life of the parent who signed the contract

6. The interest rate for an annual loan of $5,000 from the   6.___
organization described in the above passage for a student
whose family's net income was $11,000 should be
     A. 3%   B. 3.5%   C. 4%   D. 4.5%

7. The interest rate for an annual loan of $7,000 from the   7.___
organization described in the above passage for a student
whose family's net income was $20,000 should be
     A. 5%   B. 8%   C. 9%   D. 10%

8. John Lee has submitted an application for the installment   8.___
payment plan described in the above passage. John's mother
and father have a store which grossed $100,000 last year,
but the income which the family received from the store
was $18,000 before taxes. They also had $1,000 income
from stock dividends. They paid $2,000 in income taxes.
The amount of income upon which the interest should be
based is
     A. $17,000   B. $18,000   C. $19,000   D. $21,000

Questions 9-13.

DIRECTIONS: Questions 9 through 13 are to be answered SOLELY on
the basis of the following passage.

Since an organization chart is pictorial in nature, there is a
tendency for it to be drawn in an artistically balanced and appealing
fashion, regardless of the realities of actual organizational structure. In addition to being subject to this distortion, there is the
difficulty of communicating in any organization chart the relative
importance or the relative size of various component parts of an
organizational structure. Furthermore, because of the need for simplicity of design, an organization chart can never indicate the full
extent of the interrelationships among the component parts of an
organization. These interrelationships are often just as vital as the
specifications which an organization chart endeavors to indicate. Yet,
if an organization chart were to be drawn with all the wide variety of
criss-crossing communication and cooperation networks existent within
a typical organization, the chart would probably be much more con-
fusing than informative. It is also obvious that no organization
chart as such can *prove* or *disprove* that the organizational structure
it represents is effective in realizing the objectives of the organization. At best, an organization chart can only illustrate some of
the various factors to be taken into consideration in understanding,
devising, or altering organizational arrangements.

9. According to the above passage, an organization chart can   9.___
   be expected to portray the
   A. structure of the organization along somewhat ideal lines
   B. relative size of the organizational units quite
      accurately
   C. channels of information distribution within the organi-
      zation graphically
   D. extent of the obligation of each unit to meet the
      organizational objectives

10. According to the above passage, those aspects of internal   10.___
    functioning which are NOT shown on an organization chart
    A. can be considered to have little practical application
       in the operations of the organization
    B. might well be considered to be as important as the
       structural relationships which a chart does present
    C. could be the cause of considerable confusion in the
       operations of an organization which is quite large
    D. would be most likely to provide the information
       needed to determine the overall effectiveness of an
       organization

11. In the above passage, the one of the following conditions   11.___
    which is NOT implied as being a defect of an organization
    chart is that an organization chart may
    A. present a picture of the organizational structure
       which is different from the structure that actually
       exists
    B. fail to indicate the comparative size of various
       organizational units
    C. be limited in its ability to convey some of the
       meaningful aspects of organizational relationships
    D. become less useful over a period of time during
       which the organizational facts which it illustrated
       have changed

12. The one of the following which is the MOST suitable title   12.___
    for the above passage is
    A. THE DESIGN AND CONSTRUCTION OF AN ORGANIZATION CHART
    B. THE INFORMAL ASPECTS OF AN ORGANIZATION CHART
    C. THE INHERENT DEFICIENCIES OF AN ORGANIZATION CHART
    D. THE UTILIZATION OF A TYPICAL ORGANIZATION CHART

13. It can be INFERRED from the above passage that the func-   13.___
    tion of an organization chart is to
    A. contribute to the comprehension of the organization
       form and arrangements
    B. establish the capabilities of the organization to
       operate effectively
    C. provide a balanced picture of the operations of the
       organization
    D. eliminate the need for complexity in the organization's
       structure

Questions 14-16.

DIRECTIONS: Questions 14 through 16 are to be answered SOLELY on
the basis of the following passage.

In dealing with visitors to the school office, the school secretary must use initiative, tact, and good judgment. All visitors
should be greeted promptly and courteously. The nature of their
business should be determined quickly and handled expeditiously.
Frequently, the secretary should be able to handle requests, receipts,
deliveries, or passes herself. Her judgment should determine when
a visitor should see members of the staff or the principal. Serious
problems or doubtful cases should be referred to a supervisor.

14.   In general, visitors should be handled by the   14.____
      A. school secretary   B. principal
      C. appropriate supervisor   D. person who is free

15.   It is wise to obtain the following information from   15.____
      visitors:
      A. Name   B. Nature of business
      C. Address   D. Problems they have

16.   All visitors who wish to see members of the staff should   16.____
      A. be permitted to do so
      B. produce identification
      C. do so for valid reasons only
      D. be processed by a supervisor

Questions 17-19.

DIRECTIONS: Questions 17 through 19 are to be answered SOLELY on
the basis of the following passage.

Information regarding payroll status, salary differentials,
promotional salary increments, deductions, and pension payments
should be given to all members of the staff who have questions
regarding these items. On occasion, if the secretary is uncertain
regarding the information, the staff member should be referred to
the principal or the appropriate agency. No question by a staff
member regarding payroll status should be brushed aside as immaterial
or irrelevant. The school secretary must always try to handle the
question or pass it on to the person who can handle it.

17.   If a teacher is dissatisfied with information regarding   17.____
      her salary status, as given by the school secretary, the
      matter should be
      A. dropped
      B. passed on to the principal
      C. passed on by the secretary to proper agency or the
         principal
      D. made a basis for grievance procedures

18. The following is an adequate summary of the above passage: 18.____
    A. The secretary must handle all payroll matters
    B. The secretary must handle all payroll matters or know
       who can handle them
    C. The secretary or the principal must handle all payroll
       matters
    D. Payroll matters too difficult to handle must be followed
       up until they are solved

19. The above passage implies that   19.____
    A. many teachers ask immaterial questions regarding
       payroll status
    B. few teachers ask irrelevant pension questions
    C. no teachers ask immaterial salary questions
    D. no question regarding salary should be considered
       irrelevant

Questions 20-22.

DIRECTIONS: Questions 20 through 22 are to be answered SOLELY on
              the basis of the following passage.

   The necessity for good speech on the part of the school secretary
cannot be overstated. The school secretary must deal with the general
public, the pupils, the members of the staff, and the school supervisors. In every situation which involves the general public, the
secretary serves as a representative of the school. In dealing with
pupils, the secretary's speech must serve as a model from which students
may guide themselves. Slang, colloquialisms, malapropisms, and local
dialects must be avoided.

20. The above passage implies that the speech pattern of the   20.____
    secretary must be
    A. perfect
    B. very good
    C. average
    D. on a level with that of the pupils

21. The last sentence indicates that slang   21.____
    A. is acceptable
    B. occurs in all speech
    C. might be used occasionally
    D. should be shunned

22. The above passage implies that the speech of pupils   22.____
    A. may be influenced   B. does not change readily
    C. is generally good   D. is generally poor

Questions 23-25.

DIRECTIONS: Questions 23 through 25 are to be answered SOLELY on
              the basis of the following passage.

   The school secretary who is engaged in the task of filing records
and correspondence should follow a general set of rules. Items which
are filed should be available to other secretaries or to supervisors

13

quickly and easily by means of the application of a modicum of common sense and good judgment. Items which, by their nature, may be difficult to find should be cross-indexed. Folders and drawers should be neatly and accurately labeled. There should never be a large accumulation of papers which have not been filed.

23. A good general rule to follow in filing is that materials should be
    A. placed in folders quickly
    B. neatly stored
    C. readily available
    D. cross-indexed

23. ___

24. Items that are filed should be available to
    A. the secretary charged with the task of filing
    B. secretaries and supervisors
    C. school personnel
    D. the principal

24. ___

25. A modicum of common sense means _____ common sense.
    A. an average amount of   B. a great deal of
    C. a little   D. no

25. ___

TEST 3

Questions 1-4.

DIRECTIONS: Questions 1 through 4 are to be answered SOLELY on the basis of the following passage.

The proposition that administrative activity is essentially the same in all organizations appears to underlie some of the practices in the administration of private higher education. Although the practice is unusual in public education, there are numerous instances of industrial, governmental, or military administrators being assigned to private institutions of higher education and, to a lesser extent, of college and university presidents assuming administrative positions in other types of organizations. To test this theory that administrators are interchangeable, there is a need for systematic observation and classification. The myth that an educational administrator must first have experience in the teaching profession is firmly rooted in a long tradition that has historical prestige. The myth is bound up in the expectations of the public and personnel surrounding the administrator. Since administrative success depends significantly on how well an administrator meets the expectations others have of him, the myth may be more powerful than the special experience in helping the administrator attain organizational and educational objectives. Educational administrators who have risen through the teaching profession have often expressed nostalgia for the life of a teacher or scholar, but there is no evidence that this nostalgia contributes to administrative success.

1. Which of the following statements as completed is MOST   1.___
    consistent with the above passage?
    The greatest number of administrators has moved from
       A. industry and the military to government and universities
       B. government and universities to industry and the military
       C. government, the armed forces, and industry to colleges
          and universities
       D. colleges and universities to government, the armed
          forces, and industry

2. Of the following, the MOST reasonable inference from the   2.___
    above passage is that a specific area requiring further
    research is the
       A. place of myth in the tradition and history of the
          educational profession
       B. relative effectiveness of educational administrators
          from inside and outside the teaching profession
       C. performance of administrators in the administration
          of public colleges
       D. degree of reality behind the nostalgia for scholarly
          pursuits often expressed by educational administrators

3. According to the above passage, the value to an educational   3.___
    administrator of experience in the teaching profession
       A. lies in the firsthand knowledge he has acquired of
          immediate educational problems
       B. may lie in the belief of his colleagues, subordinates,
          and the public that such experience is necessary
       C. has been supported by evidence that the experience
          contributes to administrative success in educational
          fields
       D. would be greater if the administrator were able to
          free himself from nostalgia for his former duties

4. Of the following, the MOST suitable title for the above   4.___
    passage is
       A. EDUCATIONAL ADMINISTRATION, ITS PROBLEMS
       B. THE EXPERIENCE NEEDED FOR EDUCATIONAL ADMINISTRATION
       C. ADMINISTRATION IN HIGHER EDUCATION
       D. EVALUATING ADMINISTRATIVE EXPERIENCE

Questions 5-6.

DIRECTIONS: Questions 5 and 6 are to be answered SOLELY on the
             basis of the following passage.

Management by objectives (MBO) may be defined as the process by
which the superior and the subordinate managers of an organization
jointly define its common goals, define each individual's major areas
of responsibility in terms of the results expected of him and use
these measures as guides for operating the unit and assessing the
contribution of each of its members.

The MBO approach requires that after organizational goals are established and communicated, targets must be set for each individual position which are congruent with organizational goals. Periodic performance reviews and a final review using the objectives set as criteria are also basic to this approach.

Recent studies have shown that MBO programs are influenced by attitudes and perceptions of the boss, the company, the reward-punishment system, and the program itself. In addition, the manner in which the MBO program is carried out can influence the success of the program. A study done in the late sixties indicates that the best results are obtained when the manager sets goals which deal with significant problem areas in the organizational unit, or with the subordinate's personal deficiencies. These goals must be clear with regard to what is expected of the subordinate. The frequency of feedback is also important in the success of a management-by-objectives program. Generally, the greater the amount of feedback, the more successful the MBO program.

5. According to the above passage, the expected output for individual employees should be determined
   A. after a number of reviews of work performance
   B. after common organizational goals are defined
   C. before common organizational goals are defined
   D. on the basis of an employee's personal qualities

5.___

6. According to the above passage, the management-by-objectives approach requires
   A. less feedback than other types of management programs
   B. little review of on-the-job performance after the initial setting of goals
   C. general conformance between individual goals and organizational goals
   D. the setting of goals which deal with minor problem areas in the organization

6.___

Questions 7-10.

DIRECTIONS: Questions 7 through 10 are to be answered SOLELY on the basis of the following passage.

Management, which is the function of executive leadership, has as its principal phases the planning, organizing, and controlling of the activities of subordinate groups in the accomplishment of organizational objectives. Planning specifies the kind and extent of the factors, forces, and effects, and the relationships among them, that will be required for satisfactory accomplishment. The nature of the objectives and their requirements must be known before determinations can be made as to what must be done, how it must be done and why, where actions should take place, who should be responsible, and similar problems pertaining to the formulation of a plan. Organizing, which creates the conditions that must be present before the execution of the plan can be undertaken successfully, cannot be done intelligently without knowledge of the organizational objectives. Control, which has to do with the constraint and regulation of activities entering into the execution of the plan, must be exercised in accordance with the characteristics and requirements of the activities demanded by the plan.

7. The one of the following which is the MOST suitable title   7.___
   for the above passage is
   - A. THE NATURE OF SUCCESSFUL ORGANIZATION
   - B. THE PLANNING OF MANAGEMENT FUNCTIONS
   - C. THE IMPORTANCE OF ORGANIZATIONAL FUNCTIONS
   - D. THE PRINCIPLE ASPECTS OF MANAGEMENT

8. It can be inferred from the above passage that the one of   8.___
   the following functions whose existence is essential to
   the existence of the other three is the
   - A. regulation of the work needed to carry out a plan
   - B. understanding of what the organization intends to
     accomplish
   - C. securing of information of the factors necessary for
     accomplishment of objectives
   - D. establishment of the conditions required for success-
     ful action

9. The one of the following which would NOT be included   9.___
   within any of the principal phases of the function of
   executive leadership as defined in the above passage is
   - A. determination of manpower requirements
   - B. procurement of required material
   - C. establishment of organizational objectives
   - D. scheduling of production

10. The conclusion which can MOST reasonably be drawn from   10.___
    the above passage is that the control phase of managing
    is most directly concerned with the
    - A. influencing of policy determinations
    - B. administering of suggestion systems
    - C. acquisition of staff for the organization
    - D. implementation of performance standards

Questions 11-12.

DIRECTIONS: Questions 11 and 12 are to be answered SOLELY on the
basis of the following passage.

Under an open-and-above-board policy, it is to be expected that some supervisors will gloss over known shortcomings of subordinates rather than face the task of discussing them face-to-face. It is also to be expected that at least some employees whose job performance is below par will reject the supervisor's appraisal as biased and unfair. Be that as it may, these are inescapable aspects of any performance appraisal system in which human beings are involved. The supervisor who shies away from calling a spade a spade, as well as the employee with a chip on his shoulder, will each in his own way eventually be revealed in his true light -- to the benefit of the organization as a whole.

11. The BEST of the following interpretations of the above   11.___
    passage is that
    A. the method of rating employee performance requires
       immediate revision to improve employee acceptance
    B. substandard performance ratings should be discussed
       with employees even if satisfactory ratings are not
    C. supervisors run the risk of being called unfair by
       their subordinates even though their appraisals are
       accurate
    D. any system of employee performance rating is satis-
       factory if used properly

12. The BEST of the following interpretations of the above   12.___
    passage is that
    A. supervisors generally are not open-and-above-board
       with their subordinates
    B. it is necessary for supervisors to tell employees
       objectively how they are performing
    C. employees complain when their supervisor does not
       keep them informed
    D. supervisors are afraid to tell subordinates their
       weaknesses

Questions 13-15.

DIRECTIONS: Questions 13 through 15 are to be answered SOLELY on
              the basis of the following passage.

During the last decade, a great deal of interest has been
generated around the phenomenon of *organizational development*, or
the process of developing human resources through conscious organization effort. Organizational development (OD) stresses improving
interpersonal relationships and organizational skills, such as
communication, to a much greater degree than individual training
ever did.

The kind of training that an organization should emphasize
depends upon the present and future structure of the organization.
If future organizations are to be unstable, shifting coalitions,
then individual skills and abilities, particularly those emphasizing
innovativeness, creativity, flexibility, and the latest technological
knowledge, are crucial and individual training is most appropriate.

But if there is to be little change in organizational structure,
then the main thrust of training should be group-oriented or organizational development. This approach seems better designed for over-
coming hierarchical barriers, for developing a degree of interpersonal
relationships which make communication along the chain of command
possible, and for retaining a modicum of innovation and/or flexibility.

13. According to the above passage, group-oriented training   13.___
    is MOST useful in
    A. developing a communications system that will facilitate
       understanding through the chain of command
    B. highly flexible and mobile organizations

C. preventing the crossing of hierarchical barriers within an organization
D. saving energy otherwise wasted on developing methods
   of dealing with rigid hierarchies

14. The one of the following conclusions which can be drawn   14.___
    MOST appropriately from the above passage is that
    A. behavioral research supports the use of organizational
       development training methods rather than individualized
       training
    B. it is easier to provide individualized training in
       specific skills than to set up sensitivity training
       programs
    C. organizational development eliminates innovative or
       flexible activity
    D. the nature of an organization greatly influences which
       training methods will be most effective

15. According to the above passage, the one of the following   15.___
    which is LEAST important for large-scale organizations
    geared to rapid and abrupt change is
    A. current technological information
    B. development of a high degree of interpersonal
       relationships
    C. development of individual skills and abilities
    D. emphasis on creativity

Questions 16-18.

DIRECTIONS: Questions 16 through 18 are to be answered SOLELY on
              the basis of the following passage.

    The increase in the extent to which each individual is personally
responsible to others is most noticeable in a large bureaucracy. No
one person *decides* anything; each decision of any importance is the
product of an intricate process of brokerage involving individuals
inside and outside the organization who feel some reason to be affected
by the decision, or who have special knowledge to contribute to it.
The more varied the organization's constituency, the more outside *veto-
groups* will need to be taken into account. But even if no outside
consultations were involved, sheer size would produce a complex process of decision. For a large organization is a deliberately created
system of tensions into which each individual is expected to bring
work-ways,viewpoints, and outside relationships markedly different
from those of his colleagues. It is the administrator's task to draw
from these disparate forces the elements of wise action from day to
day, consistent with the purposes of the organization as a whole.

16. The above passage is ESSENTIALLY a description of decision- 16.___
    making as
    A. an organization process
    B. the key responsibility of the administrator
    C. the one best position among many
    D. a complex of individual decisions

19

17. Which one of the following statements BEST describes the   17.____
    responsibilities of an administrator?
    A. He modifies decisions and goals in accordance with
       pressures from within and outside the organization.
    B. He creates problem-solving mechanisms that rely on
       the varied interests of his staff and *veto-groups*.
    C. He makes determinations that will lead to attainment
       of his agency's objectives.
    D. He obtains agreement among varying viewpoints and
       interests.

18. In the context of the operations of a central public   18.____
    personnel agency, a *veto group* would LEAST likely consist
    of
    A. employee organizations
    B. professional personnel societies
    C. using agencies
    D. civil service newspapers

Questions 19-25.

DIRECTIONS: Questions 19 through 25 are to be answered SOLELY on
               the basis of the following passage, which is an extract
               from a report prepared for Department X, which outlines
               the procedure to be followed in the case of transfers
               of employees.

Every transfer, regardless of the reason therefor, requires completion of the record of transfer, Form DT 411. To denote consent to
the transfer, DT 411 should contain the signatures of the transferee
and the personnel officer(s) concerned, except that, in the case of
an involuntary transfer, the signatures of the transferee's present
and prospective supervisors shall be entered in Boxes 8A and 8B,
respectively, since the transferee does not consent. Only a permanent
employee may request a transfer; in such cases, the employee's attendance record shall be duly considered with regard to absences, late-
nesses, and accrued overtime balances. In the case of an inter-
district transfer, the employee's attendance record must be included
in Section 8A of the transfer request, Form DT 410, by the personnel
officer of the district from which the transfer is requested. The
personnel officer of the district to which the employee requested
transfer may refuse to accept accrued overtime balances in excess of
ten days.

An employee on probation shall be eligible for transfer. If such
employee is involuntarily transferred, he shall be credited for the
period of time already served on probation. However, if such transfer
is voluntary, the employee shall be required to serve the entire
period of his probation in the new position. An employee who has
occurred a disability which prevents him from performing his normal
duties may be transferred during the period of such disability to
other appropriate duties. A disability transfer requires the completion of either Form DT 414 if the disability is job-connected, or
Form DT 415 if it is not a job-connected disability. In either case,
the personnel officer of the district from which the transfer is made

20

signs in Box 6A of the first two copies and the personnel officer of the district to which the transfer is made signs in Box 6B of the last two copies, or, in the case of an intra-district disability transfer, the personnel officer must sign in Box 6A of the first two copies and Box 6B of the last two copies.

19. When a personnel officer consents to an employee's request   19.___
    for transfer from his district, this procedure requires
    that the personnel officer sign Form(s)
    A. DT 411
    B. DT 410 and DT 411
    C. DT 411 and either Form DT 414 or DT 415
    D. DT 410 and DT 411, and either Form DT 414 or DT 415

20. With respect to the time record of an employee transferred   20.___
    against his wishes during his probationary period, this
    procedure requires that
    A. he serve the entire period of his probation in his
       present office
    B. he lose his accrued overtime balance
    C. his attendance record be considered with regard to
       absences and latenesses
    D. he be given credit for the period of time he has
       already served on probation

21. Assume you are a supervisor and an employee must be trans-   21.___
    ferred into your office against his wishes.
    According to the this procedure, the box you must sign on
    the record of transfer is
    A. 6A   B. 8A   C. 6B   D. 8B

22. Under this procedure, in the case of a disability trans-   22.___
    fer, when must Box 6A on Forms DT 414 and DT 415 be signed
    by the personnel officer of the district to which the
    transfer is being made?
    A. In all cases when either Form DT 414 or Form DT 415
       is used
    B. In all cases when Form DT 414 is used and only under
       certain circumstances when Form DT 415 is used
    C. In all cases when Form DT 415 is used and only under
       certain circumstances when Form DT 414 is used
    D. Only under certain circumstances when either Form
       DT 414 or Form DT 415 is used

23. From the above passage, it may be inferred MOST correctly   23.___
    that the number of copies of Form DT 414 is
    A. no more than 2
    B. at least 3
    C. at least 5
    D. more than the number of copies of Form DT 415

24. A change in punctuation and capitalization only which   24.___
    would change one sentence into two and possibly contribute
    to somewhat greater ease of reading this report extract
    would be MOST appropriate in the
    A. 2nd sentence, 1st paragraph
    B. 3rd sentence, 1st paragraph

21

C. next to the last sentence, 2nd paragraph
D. 2nd sentence, 2nd paragraph

25. In the second paragraph, a word that is INCORRECTED used   25._____
    is
    A. *shall* in the 1st sentence
    B. *voluntary* in the 3rd sentence
    C. *occurred* in the 4th sentence
    D. *intra-district* in the last sentence

KEY (CORRECT ANSWERS)

TEST 1	TEST 2	TEST 3
1. D	1. B	1. C
2. C	2. A	2. B
3. D	3. C	3. B
4. B	4. C	4. B
5. A	5. D	5. B
6. A	6. B	6. C
7. C	7. B	7. D
8. C	8. C	8. B
9. A	9. A	9. C
10. B	10. B	10. D
11. D	11. D	11. C
12. A	12. C	12. B
13. A	13. A	13. A
14. C	14. A	14. D
15. D	15. B	15. B
16. A	16. C	16. A
17. D	17. C	17. C
18. B	18. B	18. B
19. C	19. D	19. A
20. D	20. B	20. D
21. D	21. D	21. D
22. D	22. A	22. D
23. A	23. C	23. B
24. B	24. B	24. B
25. C	25. C	25. C

SPELLING
EXAMINATION SECTION
TEST 1

DIRECTIONS: In each of the following tests in this part, select the letter of the one MISSPELLED word in each of the following groups of words. *PRINT THE LETTER OF THE CORRECT ANSWER IN THE SPACE AT THE RIGHT.*

1. A. grateful   B. fundimental   1.___
    C. census   D. analysis

2. A. installment   B. retrieve   2.___
    C. concede   D. dissapear

3. A. accidentaly   B. dismissal   3.___
    C. conscientious D. indelible

4. A. perceive   B. carreer   C. anticipate   D. acquire   4.___

5. A. facillity   B. reimburse C. assortment   D. guidance   5.___

6. A. plentiful   B. across   6.___
    C. advantagous   D. similar

7. A. omission   B. pamphlet   C. guarrantee   D. repel   7.___

8. A. maintenance   B. always   8.___
    C. liable   D. anouncement

9. A. exaggerate B. sieze   C. condemn   D. commit   9.___

10. A. pospone   B. altogether C. grievance   D. excessive 10.___

11. A. banana   B. trafic   C. spectacle   D. boundary   11.___

12. A. commentator   B. abbreviation   12.___
    C. battaries   D. monastery

13. A. practically   B. advise   13.___
    C. pursuade   D. laboratory

14. A. fatigueing   B. invincible   14.___
    C. strenuous   D. ceiling

15. A. propeller   B. reverence C. piecemeal   D. underneth 15.___

16. A. annonymous B. envelope   C. transit   D. variable   16.___

17. A. petroleum   B. bigoted   C. meager   D. resistence 17.___

18. A. permissible   B. indictment   18.___
    C. fundamental   D. nowadays

| 19. | A. thief | B. bargin | C. nuisance | D. vacant | 19.___ |
| 20. | A. technique | B. vengeance | C. aquatic | D. heighth | 20.___ |

TEST 2

1.	A. apparent	B. superintendent			1.___
	C. releive	D. calendar			
2.	A. foreign	B. negotiate	C. typical	D. disipline	2.___
3.	A. posponed	B. argument			3.___
	C. susceptible	D. deficit			
4.	A. preferred	B. column	C. peculiar	D. equiped	4.___
5.	A. exaggerate	B. disatisfied			5.___
	C. repetition	D. already			
6.	A. livelihood	B. physician	C. obsticle	D. strategy	6.___
7.	A. courageous	B. ommission	C. ridiculous	D. awkward	7.___
8.	A. sincerely	B. abundance	C. negligable	D. elementary	8.___
9.	A. obsolete	B. mischievous			9.___
	C. enumerate	D. atheletic			
10.	A. fiscel	B. beneficiary			10.___
	C. concede	D. translate			
11.	A. segregate	B. excessivly	C. territory	D. obstacle	11.___
12.	A. unnecessary	B. monopolys			12.___
	C. harmonious	D. privilege			
13.	A. sinthetic	B. intellectual			13.___
	C. gracious	D. archaic			
14.	A. beneficial	B. fulfill	C. sarcastic	D. disolve	14.___
15.	A. umbrella	B. sentimental			15.___
	C. inefficent	D. psychiatrist			
16.	A. noticable	B. knapsack	C. librarian	D. meant	16.___
17.	A. conference	B. upheaval	C. vulger	D. odor	17.___
18.	A. surmount	B. pentagon	C. calorie	D. inumerable	18.___
19.	A. classifiable	B. moisturize			19.___
	C. monitor	D. assesment			
20.	A. thermastat	B. corrupting	C. approach	D. thinness	20.___

TEST 3

1. A. typical   B. descend   C. summarize   D. continuel   1.___

2. A. courageous   B. recomend   C. omission   D. eliminate   2.___

3. A. compliment   B. illuminate   3.___
    C. auxilary   D. installation

4. A. preliminary   B. aquainted   4.___
    C. syllable   D. analysis

5. A. accustomed   B. negligible   C. interupted   D. bulletin   5.___

6. A. summoned   B. managment   C. mechanism   D. sequence   6.___

7. A. commitee   B. surprise   C. noticeable   D. emphasize   7.___

8. A. occurrance   B. likely   C. accumulate   D. grievance   8.___

9. A. obstacle   B. particuliar   9.___
    C. baggage   D. fascinating

10. A. innumerable   B. seize   10.___
    C. applicant   D. dictionery

11. A. monkeys   B. rigid   C. unnatural   D. roomate   11.___

12. A. surveying   B. figurative   C. famous   D. curiosety   12.___

13. A. rodeo   B. inconcievable   13.___
    C. calendar   D. magnificence

14. A. handicaped   B. glacier   C. defiance   D. emperor   14.___

15. A. schedule   B. scrawl   C. seclusion   D. sissors   15.___

16. A. tissues   B. tomatos   C. tyrants   D. tragedies   16.___

17. A. casette   B. graceful   C. penicillin   D. probably   17.___

18. A. gnawed   B. microphone   C. clinicle   D. batch   18.___

19. A. amateur   B. altitude   C. laborer   D. expence   19.___

20. A. mandate   B. flexable   C. despise   D. verify   20.___

TEST 4

1. A. primery   B. mechanic   C. referred   D. admissible   1.___

2. A. cessation   B. beleif   C. aggressive   D. allowance   2.___

3. A. leisure   B. authentic   3.___
    C. familiar   D. contemptable

3

4. A. volume   B. forty   C. dilemma   D. seldum   4.___

5. A. discrepancy   B. aquisition   5.___
    C. exorbitant   D. lenient

6. A. simultanous   B. penetrate   6.___
    C. revision   D. conspicuous

7. A. ilegible   B. gracious   C. profitable D. obedience   7.___

8. A. manufacturer   B. authorize   8.___
    C. compelling   D. pecular

9. A. anxious   B. rehearsal   C. handicaped D. tendency   9.___

10. A. meticulous   B. accompaning   10.___
    C. initiative   D. shelves

11. A. hammaring   B. insecticide   11.___
    C. capacity   D. illogical

12. A. budget   B. luminous   C. aviation   D. lunchon   12.___

13. A. moniter   B. bachelor   13.___
    C. pleasurable   D. omitted

14. A. monstrous   B. transistor   C. narrative   D. anziety   14.___

15. A. engagement   B. judical   C. pasteurize D. tried   15.___

16. A. fundimental   B. innovation   16.___
    C. perpendicular   D. extravagant

17. A. bookkeeper   B. brutality   C. gymnaseum   D. cemetery   17.___

18. A. sturdily   B. pretentious   18.___
    C. gourmet   D. enterance

19. A. resturant   B. tyranny   19.___
    C. kindergarten   D. ancestry

20. A. benefit   B. possess   C. speciman   D. noticing   20.___

TEST 5

1. A. arguing   B. correspondance   1.___
    C. forfeit   D. dissension

2. A. occasion   B. description   2.___
    C. prejudice   D. elegible

3. A. accomodate   B. initiative   C. changeable D. enroll   3.___

4. A. temporary   B. insistent   C. benificial   D. separate   4.___

5. A. achieve   B. dissappoint   5.___
    C. unanimous   D. judgment

6. A. procede   B. publicly   C. sincerity   D. successful   6.___

7. A. deceive   B. goverment   C. preferable   D. repetitive   7.___

8. A. emphasis   B. skillful   C. advisible   D. optimistic   8.___

9. A. tendency   B. rescind   C. crucial   D. noticable   9.___

10. A. privelege   B. abbreviate   C. simplify   D. divisible   10.___

11. A. irresistible   B. varius   11.___
    C. mutual   D. refrigerator

12. A. amateur   B. distinguish   12.___
    C. rehearsal   D. poision

13. A. biased   B. ommission   C. precious   D. coordinate   13.___

14. A. calculated   B.enthusiasm   C. sincerely   D. parashute   14.___

15. A. sentry   B. materials   C. incredable   D. budget   15.___

16. A. chocolate   B. instrument   C. volcanoe   D. shoulder   16.___

17. A. ancestry   B. obscure   C. intention   D. ninty   17.___

18. A. artical   B. bracelet   C. beggar   D. hopeful   18.___

19. A. tournament   B. sponsor   19.___
    C. perpendiclar   D. dissolve

20. A. yeild   B. physician   C. greasiest   D. admitting   20.___

TEST 6

1. A. achievment   B. maintenance   1.___
    C. questionnaire   D. all are correct

2. A. prevelant   B. pronunciation   2.___
    C. separate   D. all are correct

3. A. permissible   B. relevant   3.___
    C. seize   D. all are correct

4. A. corroborate   B. desparate   4.___
    C. eighth   D. all are correct

5. A. exceed   B. feasibility   5.___
    C. psycological   D. all are correct

6. A. parallel   B. aluminum   C. calendar   D. eigty   6.___

7. A. microbe   B. ancient   C. autograph D. existance 7.___

8. A. plentiful B. skillful   C. amoung   D. capsule   8.___

9. A. erupt   B. quanity   C. opinion   D. competent 9.___

10. A. excitement B. discipline C. luncheon   D. regreting 10.___

11. A. magazine   B. expository C. imitation D. permenent 11.___

12. A. ferosious   B. machinery   12.___
    C. precise   D. magnificent

13. A. conceive   B. narritive C. separation D. management 13.___

14. A. muscular   B. witholding C. pickle   D. glacier   14.___

15. A. vehicel   B. mismanage   15.___
    C. correspondence   D. dissatisfy

16. A. sentince   B. bulletin   C. notice   D. definition 16.___

17. A. appointment   B. exactly   17.___
    C. typest   D. light

18. A. penalty   B. suparvise C. consider   D. division   18.___

19. A. schedule   B. accurate   C. corect   D. simple   19.___

20. A. suggestion B. installed C. proper   D. agincy   20.___

TEST 7

1. A. symtom   B. serum   C. antiseptic D. aromatic   1.___

2. A. register   B. registrar C. purser   D. burser   2.___

3. A. athletic   B. tragedy   C. batallion D. sophomore 3.___

4. A. latent   B. godess   C. aisle   D. whose   4.___

5. A. rhyme   B. rhythm   C. thime   D. thine   5.___

6. A. eighth   B. exaggerate C. electorial D. villain   6.___

7. A. statute   B. superintendent   7.___
    C. iresistible   D. colleague

8. A. sieze   B. therefor   C. auxiliary   D. changeable   8.____

9. A. siege   B. knowledge   C. lieutenent   D. weird   9.____

10. A. acquitted   B. polititian   C. professor   D. conqueror   10.____

11. A. changeable   B. chargeable   C. salable   D. useable   11.____

12. A. promissory   B. prisoner   C. excellent   D. tyrany   12.____

13. A. conspicuous   B. essance   13.____
    C. comparative   D. brilliant

14. A. notefying   B. accentuate   C. adhesive   D. primarily   14.____

15. A. exercise   B. sublime   C. stuborn   D. shameful   15.____

16. A. presume   B. transcript   C. strech   D. wizard   16.____

17. A. specify   B. regional   17.____
    C. arbitrary   D. segragation

18. A. requirement   B. happiness   18.____
    C. achievement   D. gentlely

19. A. endurance   B. fusion   C. balloon   D. enormus   19.____

20. A. luckily   B. schedule   C. simplicity   D. sanwich   20.____

TEST 8

1. A. maintain   B. maintainance   1.____
    C. sustain   D. sustenance

2. A. portend   B. portentious   2.____
    C. pretend   D. pretentious

3. A. prophesize   B. prophesies   3.____
    C. farinaceous   D. spaceous

4. A. choose   B. chose   C. choosen   D. chasten   4.____

5. A. censure   B. censorious   5.____
    C. pleasure   D. pleasurible

6. A. cover   B. coverage   C. adder   D. adege   6.____

7. A. balloon   B. diregible   C. direct   D. descent   7.____

8. A. whemsy   B. crazy   C. flimsy   D. lazy   8.____

9. A. derision   B. pretention   C. sustention   D. contention   9.____

10. A. question   B. questionaire   10. ___
     C. legion   D. legionary

11. A. chattle   B. cattle   C. dismantle   D. kindle   11. ___

12. A. canal   B. cannel   C. chanel   D. colonel   12. ___

13. A. hemorrage B. storage   C. manage   D. foliage   13. ___

14. A. surgeon   B. sturgeon C. luncheon   D. stancheon   14. ___

15. A. diploma   B. commission C. dependent   D. luminious   15. ___

16. A. likelihood B. blizzard C. machanical   D. suppress   16. ___

17. A. commercial B. releif   C. disposal   D. endeavor   17. ___

18. A. operate   B. bronco   C. excaping   D. grammar   18. ___

19. A. orchard   B. collar   C. embarass   D. distant   19. ___

20. A. sincerly   B. possessive C. weighed   D. waist   20. ___

TEST 9

1. A. statute   B. stationary   1. ___
    C. staturesque   D. stature

2. A. practicible   B. practical   2. ___
    C. particle   D. reticule

3. A. plague   B. plaque   C. ague   D. aigrete   3. ___

4. A. theology B. idealogy   C. psychology D. philology   4. ___

5. A. dilema   B. stamina   C. feminine D. strychnine   5. ___

6. A. deceit   B. benefit   C. grieve   D. hienous   6. ___

7. A. commensurable   B. measurable   7. ___
    C. duteable   D. salable

8. A. homogeneous   B. heterogeneous   8. ___
    C. advantageous   D. religeous

9. A. criticize B. dramatise C. exorcise D. exercise   9. ___

10. A. ridiculous B. comparable C. merciful D. cotten   10. ___

11. A. antebiotic B. stitches C. pitiful   D. sneaky   11. ___

12. A. amendment   B. candadate   12. ___
    C. accountable   D. recommendation

8

13.   A. avocado   B. recruit   C. tripping   D. probally   13.___

14.   A. calendar   B. desirable   C. familar   D. vacuum   14.___

15.   A. deteriorate   B. elligible   15.___
     C. liable   D. missile

16.   A. amateur   B. competent   16.___
     C. mischeivous   D. occasion

17.   A. friendliness   B. saleries   17.___
     C. cruelty   D. ammunition

18.   A. wholesome   B. cieling   C. stupidity   D. eligible   18.___

19.   A. comptroller   B. traveled   19.___
     C. accede   D. procede

20.   A. Britain   B. Brittainica   20.___
     C. conductor   D. vendor

TEST 10

1.   A. lengthen   B. region   C. gases   D. inspecter   1.___

2.   A. imediately   B. forbidden   2.___
     C. complimentary   D. aeronautics

3.   A. continuous   B. paralel   C. opposite   D. definite   3.___

4.   A. Antarctic   B. Wednesday   C. Febuary   D. Hungary   4.___

5.   A. transmission   B. exposure   5.___
     C. pistol   D. customery

6.   A. juvinile   B. martyr   6.___
     C. deceive   D. collaborate

7.   A. unnecessary   B. repetitive   7.___
     C. cancellation   D. airey

8.   A. transit   B. availible   C. objection   D. galaxy   8.___

9.   A. ineffective   B. believeable   9.___
     C. arrangement   D. aggravate

10.   A. possession   B. progress   C. reception   D. predjudice   10.___

11.   A. congradulate   B. percolate   11.___
     C. major   D. leisure

12.   A. convenience   B. privilige   12.___
     C. emerge   D. immerse

13.   A. erasable   B. inflammable   13.___
      C. audable   D. laudable

14.   A. final   B. fines   C. finis   D. Finish   14.___

15.   A. emitted   B. representative   15.___
      C. discipline   D. insistance

16.   A. diphthong   B. rarified   C. library   D. recommend   16.___

17.   A. compel   B. belligerent   17.___
      C. successful   D. sargeant

18.   A. dispatch   B. dispise   C. dispose   D. dispute   18.___

19.   A. administrator   B. adviser   19.___
      C. diner   D. celluler

20.   A. ignite   B. ignision   C. igneous   D. ignited   20.___

TEST 11

1.   A. repellent   B. secession   C. sebaceous   D. saxaphone   1.___

2.   A. navel   B. counteresolution   2.___
      C. marginalia   D. perceptible

3.   A. Hammerskjold   B. Nehru   3.___
      C. U Thamt   D. Khrushchev

4.   A. perculate   B. periwinkle   4.___
      C. perigee   D. retrogression

5.   A. buccaneer   B. tobacco   C. Buffalo   D. oscilate   5.___

6.   A. siege   B. wierd   C. seize   D. cemetery   6.___

7.   A. equaled   B. bigoted   7.___
      C. benefited   D. kaleideoscope

8.   A. blamable   B. bullrush   8.___
      C. questionnaire   D. irascible

9.   A. tobagganed   B. acquiline   9.___
      C. capillary   D. cretonne

10.   A. daguerrotype   B. elegiacal   10.___
      C. iridescent   D. inchoate

11.   A. bayonet   B. braggadocio   11.___
      C. corollary   D. connoiseur

12.   A. equinoctial   B. fusillade   12.___
     C. fricassee   D. potpouri

13.   A. octameter   B. impressario   13.___
     C. hyetology   D. hieroglyphics

14.   A. innanity   B. idyllic   C. fylfot   D. inimical   14.___

15.   A. liquefy   B. rarefy   C. putrify   D. sapphire   15.___

16.   A. canonical   B. stupified   16.___
     C. millennium   D. memorabilia

17.   A. paraphenalia   B. odyssey   17.___
     C. onomatopoeia   D. osseous

18.   A. peregrinate   B. pecadillo   18.___
     C. reptilian   D. uxorious

19.   A. pharisaical   B. vicissitude   19.___
     C. puissance   D. wainright

20.   A. holocaust   B. tesselate   C. scintilla   D. staccato   20.___

TEST 12

1.   A. questionnaire   B. gondoleer   1.___
     C. chandelier   D. acquiescence

2.   A. surveillence   B. surfeit   2.___
     C. vaccinate   D. belligerent

3.   A. occassionally   B. recurrence   3.___
     C. silhouette   D. incessant

4.   A. transferral   B. benefical   4.___
     C. descendent   D. dependent

5.   A. separately   B. flouresence   5.___
     C. deterrent   D. parallel

6.   A. acquittal   B. enforceable   6.___
     C. counterfeit   D. indispensible

7.   A. susceptible   B. accelarate   7.___
     C. exhilarate   D. accommodation

8.   A. impedimenta   B. collateral   8.___
     C. liason   D. epistolary

9.   A. inveigle   B. panegyric   C. reservoir   D. manuver   9.___

10.   A. synopsis   B. parephernalia   10.___
      C. affidavit   D. subpoena

11.   A. grosgrain   B. vermilion   C. abbatoir   D. connoiseur   11.___

12.   A. gabardine   B. camoflage   C. hemorrhage   D. contraband   12.___

13.   A. opprobrious   B. defalcate   13.___
      C. fiduciery   D. recommendations

14.   A. nebulous   B. necessitate   14.___
      C. impricate   D. discrepancy

15.   A. discrete   B. condesension   15.___
      C. condign   D. condiment

16.   A. cavalier   B. effigy   16.___
      C. legitimatly   D. misalliance

17.   A. rheumatism   B. vaporous   17.___
      C. cannister   D. hallucinations

18.   A. paleonthology   B. octogenarian   18.___
      C. gradient   D. impingement

19.   A. fusilade   B. fusilage   C. ensilage   D. desiccate   19.___

20.   A. rationale   B. raspberry   C. reprobate   D. varigated   20.___

KEY (CORRECT ANSWERS)

TEST 1

1. B. fundamental
2. D. disappear
3. A. accidentally
4. B. career
5. A. facility

6. C. advantageous
7. C. guarantee
8. D. announcement
9. B. seize
10. A. postpone

11. B. traffic
12. C. batteries
13. C. persuade
14. A. fatiguing
15. D. underneath

16. A. anonymous
17. D. resistance
18. C. fundamental
19. B. bargain
20. D. height

TEST 2

1. C. relieve
2. D. discipline
3. A. postponed
4. D. equipped
5. B. dissatisfied

6. C. obstacle
7. B. omission
8. C. negligible
9. D. athletic
10. A. fiscal

11. B. excessively
12. B. monopolies
13. A. synthetic
14. D. dissolve
15. C. inefficient

16. A. noticeable
17. C. vulgar
18. D. innumerable
19. D. assessment
20. A. thermostat

TEST 3

1. D. continual
2. B. recommend
3. C. auxiliary
4. B. acquainted
5. C. interrupted

6. B. management
7. A. committee
8. A. occurrence
9. B. particular
10. D. dictionary

11. D. roommate
12. D. curiosity
13. B. inconceivable
14. A. handicapped
15. D. scissors

16. B. tomatoes
17. A. cassette
18. C. clinical
19. D. expense
20. B. flexible

TEST 4

1. A. primary
2. B. belief
3. D. contemptible
4. D. seldom
5. B. acquisition

6. A. simultaneous
7. A. illegible
8. D. peculiar
9. C. handicapped
10. B. accompanying

11. A. hammering
12. D. luncheon
13. A. monitor
14. D. anxiety
15. B. judicial

16. A. fundamental
17. C. gymnasium
18. D. entrance
19. A. restaurant
20. C. specimen

TEST 5

1. B. correspondence
2. D. eligible
3. A. accommodate
4. C. beneficial
5. B. disappoint

6. A. proceed
7. B. government
8. C. advisable
9. D. noticeable
10. A. privilege

11. B. various
12. D. poison
13. B. omission
14. D. parachute
15. C. incredible

16. C. volcano
17. D. ninety
18. A. article
19. C. perpendicular
20. A. yield

TEST 6

1. A. achievement
2. A. prevalent
3. D all are correct
4. B. desperate
5. C. psychological

6. D. eighty
7. D. existence
8. C. among
9. B. quantity
10. D. regretting

11. D. permanent
12. A. ferocious
13. B. narrative
14. B. withholding
15. A. vehicle

16. A. sentence
17. C. typist
18. B. supervise
19. C. correct
20. D. agency

TEST 7

1. A. symptom
2. D. bursar
3. C. battalion
4. B. goddess
5. C. thyme

6. C. electoral
7. C. irresistible
8. A. seize
9. C. lieutenant
10. B. politician

11. D. usable
12. D. tyrany
13. B. essence
14. A. notifying
15. C. stubborn

16. C. stretch
17. D. segregation
18. D. gently
19. D. enormous
20. D. sandwich

TEST 8

1. B. maintenance
2. B. portentous
3. D. spacious
4. C. chosen
5. D. pleasurable

6. D. adage
7. B. dirigible
8. A. whimsy
9. B. pretension
10. B. questionnaire

11. A. chattel
12. C. channel
13. A. hemorrhage
14. D. stanchion
15. D. luminous

16. C. mechanical
17. B. relief
18. C. escaping
19. C. embarrass
20. A. sincerely

TEST 9

1. C. statuesque
2. A. practicable
3. D. aigrette
4. B. ideology
5. A. dilemma

6. D. heinous
7. C. dutiable
8. D. religious
9. B. dramatize
10. D. cotton

11. A. antibiotic
12. B. candidate
13. D. probably
14. C. familiar
15. B. eligible

16. C. mischievous
17. B. salaries
18. B. ceiling
19. D. proceed
20. B. Brittanica

TEST 10

1. D. inspector
2. A. immediately
3. B. parallel
4. C. February
5. D. customary

6. A. juvenile
7. D. airy
8. B. available
9. B. believable
10. D. prejudice

11. A. congratulate
12. B. privilege
13. C. audible
14. D. Finnish
15. D. insistence

16. B. rarefied
17. D. sergeant
18. B. despise
19. D. cellular
20. B. ignition

TEST 11

1. D. saxophone
2. B. counterresolution
3. C. U Thant
4. A. percolate
5. D. oscillate

6. B. weird
7. D. kaleidoscope
8. B. bulrush
9. B. aquiline
10. A. daguerreotype

11. D. connoisseur
12. D. potpourri
13. B. impresario
14. A. inanity
15. C. putrefy

16. B. stupefied
17. A. paraphernalia
18. B. peccadillo
19. D. wainwright
20. B. tessellate

TEST 12

1. B. gondolier
2. A. surveillance
3. A. occasionally
4. B. beneficial
5. B. fluorescence

6. D. indispensable
7. B. accelerate
8. C. liaison
9. D. maneuver
10. B. paraphernalia

11. D. connoisseur
12. B. camouflage
13. C. fiduciary
14. C. imprecate
15. B. condescension

16. C. legitimately
17. C. canister
18. A. paleontology
19. A. fusillade
20. D. variegated

PREPARING WRITTEN MATERIAL

PARAGRAPH REARRANGEMENT

COMMENTARY

The sentences which follow are in scrambled order. You are to rearrange them in proper order and indicate the letter choice containing the correct answer at the space at the right.

Each group of sentences in this section is actually a paragraph presented in scrambled order. Each sentence in the group has a place in that paragraph; no sentence is to be left out. You are to read each group of sentences and decide upon the best order in which to put the sentences so as to form as well-organized paragraph.

The questions in this section measure the ability to solve a problem when all the facts relevant to its solution are not given.

More specifically, certain positions of responsibility and authority require the employee to discover connections between events sometimes, apparently, unrelated. In order to do this, the employee will find it necessary to correctly infer that unspecified events have probably occurred or are likely to occur. This ability becomes especially important when action must be taken on incomplete information.

Accordingly, these questions require competitors to choose among several suggested alternatives, each of which presents a different sequential arrangement of the events. Competitors must choose the MOST logical of the suggested sequences.

In order to do so, they may be required to draw on general knowledge to infer missing concepts or events that are essential to sequencing the given events. Competitors should be careful to infer only what is essential to the sequence. The plausibility of the wrong alternatives will always require the inclusion of unlikely events or of additional chains of events which are NOT essential to sequencing the given events.

It's very important to remember that you are looking for the best of the four possible choices, and that the best choice of all may not even be one of the answers you're given to choose from.

There is no one right way to these problems. Many people have found it helpful to first write out the order of the sentences, as they would have arranged them, on their scrap paper before looking at the possible answers. If their optimum answer is there, this can save them some time. If it isn't, this method can still give insight into solving the problem. Others find it most helpful to just go through each of the possible choices, contrasting each as they go along. You should use whatever method feels comfortable, and works, for you.

While most of these types of questions are not that difficult, we've added a higher percentage of the difficult type, just to give you more practice. Usually there are only one or two questions on this section that contain such subtle distinctions that you're unable to answer confidently, and you then may find yourself stuck deciding between two possible choices, neither of which you're sure about.

EXAMINATION SECTION
TEST 1

DIRECTIONS: The following groups of sentences need to be arranged in an order that makes sense. Select the letter preceding the sequence that represents the BEST sentence order. *PRINT THE LETTER OF THE CORRECT ANSWER IN THE SPACE AT THE RIGHT.*

1.   I. The keyboard was purposely designed to be a little awkward to slow typists down.
  II. The arrangement of letters on the keyboard of a typewriter was not designed for the convenience of the typist.
III. Fortunately, no one is suggesting that a new keyboard be designed right away.
 IV. If one were, we would have to learn to type all over again.
  V. The reason was that the early machines were slower than the typists and would jam easily.

  A. I, III, IV, II, V   B. II, V, I, IV, III
  C. V, I, II, III, IV   D. II, I, V, III, IV

1.___

2.   I. The majority of the new service jobs are part-time or low-paying.
  II. According to the U.S. Bureau of Labor Statistics, jobs in the service sector constitute 72% of all jobs in this country.
III. If more and more workers receive less and less money, who will buy the goods and services needed to keep the economy going?
 IV. The service sector is by far the fastest growing part of the United States economy.
  V. Some economists look upon this trend with great concern.

  A. II, IV, I, V, III   B. II, III, IV, I, V
  C. V, IV, II, III, I   D. III, I, II, IV, V

2.___

3.   I. They can also affect one's endurance.
  II. This can stabilize blood sugar levels, and ensure that the brain is receiving a steady, constant supply of glucose, so that one is *hitting on all cylinders* while taking the test.
III. By food, we mean real food, not junk food or unhealthy snacks.
 IV. For this reason, it is important not to skip a meal, and to bring food with you to the exam.
  V. One's blood sugar levels can affect how clearly one is able to think and concentrate during an exam.

  A. V, IV, II, III, I   B. V, II, I, IV, III
  C. V, I, IV, III, II   D. V, IV, I, III, II

3.___

4.
    I. Those who are the embodiment of desire are absorbed in material quests, and those who are the embodiment of feeling are warriors who value power more than possession.
    II. These qualities are in everyone, but in different degrees.
    III. But those who value understanding yearn not for goods or victory, but for knowledge.
    IV. According to Plato, human behavior flows from three main sources: desire, emotion, and knowledge.
    V. In the perfect state, the industrial forces would produce but not rule, the military would protect but not rule, and the forces of knowledge, the philosopher kings, would reign.

4.___

    A. IV, V, I, II, III   B. V, I, II, III, IV
    C. IV, III, II, I, V   D. IV, II, I, III, V

5.
    I. Of the more than 26,000 tons of garbage produced daily in New York City, 12,000 tons arrive daily at Fresh Kills.
    II. In a month, enough garbage accumulates there to fill the Empire State Building.
    III. In 1937, the Supreme Court halted the practice of dumping the trash of New York City into the sea.
    IV. Although the garbage is compacted, in a few years the mounds of garbage at Fresh Kills will be the highest points south of Maine's Mount Desert Island on the Eastern Seaboard.
    V. Instead, tugboats now pull barges of much of the trash to Staten Island and the largest landfill in the world, Fresh Kills.

5.___

    A. III, V, IV, I, II   B. III, V, II, IV, I
    C. III, V, I, II, IV   D. III, II, V, IV, I

6.
    I. Communists rank equality very high, but freedom very low.
    II. Unlike communists, conservatives place a high value on freedom and a very low value on equality.
    III. A recent study demonstrated that one way to classify people's political beliefs is to look at the importance placed on two words: freedom and equality.
    IV. Thus, by demonstrating how members of these groups feel about the two words, the study has proved to be useful for political analysts in several European countries.
    V. According to the study, socialists and liberals rank both freedom and equality very high, while fascists rate both very low.

6.___

    A. III, V, I, II, IV   B. III, IV, V, I, II
    C. III, V, IV, II, I   D. III, I, II, IV, V

7.   I. "Can there be anything more amazing than this?"   7.___
     II. If the riddle is successfully answered, his dead
         brothers will be brought back to life.
    III. "Even though man sees those around him dying every
         day," says Dharmaraj, "he still believes and acts as
         if he were immortal."
     IV. "What is the cause of ceaseless wonder?" asks the
         Lord of the Lake.
      V. In the ancient epic, The Mahabharata, a riddle is
         asked of one of the Pandava brothers.

     A. V, II, I, IV, III   B. V, IV, III, I, II
     C. V, II, IV, III, I   D. V, II, IV, I, III

8.   I. On the contrary, the two main theories -- the   8.___
         cooperative (neoclassical) theory and the radical
         (labor theory) -- clearly rest on very different
         assumptions, which have very different ethical
         overtones.
     II. The distribution of income is the primary factor in
         determining the relative levels of material well-
         being that different groups or individuals attain.
    III. Of all issues in economics, the distribution of
         income is one of the most controversial.
     IV. The neoclassical theory tends to support the existing
         income distribution (or minor changes), while the
         labor theory tends to support substantial changes in
         the way income is distributed.
      V. The intensity of the controversy reflects the fact
         that different economic theories are not purely
         neutral, *detached* theories with no ethical or moral
         implications.

     A. II, I, V, IV, III   B. III, II, V, I, IV
     C. III, V, II, I, IV   D. III, V, IV, I, II

9.   I. The pool acts as a broker and ensures that the   9.___
         cheapest power gets used first.
     II. Every six seconds, the pool's computer monitors all
         of the generating stations in the state and decides
         which to ask for more power and which to cut back.
    III. The buying and selling of electrical power is handled
         by the New York Power Pool in Guilderland, New York.
     IV. This is to the advantage of both the buying and
         selling utilities.
      V. The pool began operation in 1970, and consists of
         the state's eight electric utilities.

     A. V, I, II, III, IV   B. IV, II, I, III, V
     C. III, V, I, IV, II   D. V, III, IV, II, I

10.   I. Modern English is much simpler grammatically than
          Old English.
      II. Finnish grammar is very complicated; there are some
          fifteen cases, for example.
     III. Chinese, a very old language, may seem to be the
          exception, but it is the great number of characters/
          words that must be mastered that makes it so
          difficult to learn, not its grammar.
      IV. The newest literary language -- that is, written as
          well as spoken -- is Finnish, whose literary roots
          go back only to about the middle of the nineteenth
          century.
       V. Contrary to popular belief, the longer a language is
          been in use the simpler its grammar -- not the
          reverse.

       A. IV, I, II, III, V   B. V, I, IV, II, III
       C. I, II, IV, III, V   D. IV, II, III, I, V

10.___

KEY (CORRECT ANSWERS)

1. D	6. A
2. A	7. C
3. C	8. B
4. D	9. C
5. C	10. B

TEST 2

DIRECTIONS: This type of question tests your ability to recognize accurate paraphrasing, well-constructed paragraphs, and appropriate style and tone. It is important that the answer you select contains only the facts or concepts given in the original sentences. It is also important that you be aware of incomplete sentences, inappropriate transitions, unsupported opinions, incorrect usage, and illogical sentence order. Paragraphs that do not include all the necessary facts and concepts, that distort them, or that add new ones are not considered correct.

The format for this section may vary. Sometimes, long paragraphs are given, and emphasis is placed on style and organization. Our first five questions are of this type. Other times, the paragraphs are shorter, and there is less emphasis on style and more emphasis on accurate representation of information. Our second group of five questions are of this nature.

For each of Questions 1 through 10, select the paragraph that BEST expresses the ideas contained in the sentences above it. *PRINT THE LETTER OF THE CORRECT ANSWER IN THE SPACE AT THE RIGHT.*

1.   I. Listening skills are very important for managers.   1.___
    II. Listening skills are not usually emphasized.
   III. Whenever managers are depicted in books, manuals or the media, they are always talking, never listening.
    IV. We'd like you to read the enclosed handout on listening skills and to try to consciously apply them this week.
     V. We guarantee they will improve the quality of your interactions.

   A. Unfortunately, listening skills are not usually emphasized for managers. Managers are always depicted as talking, never listening. We'd like you to read the enclosed handout on listening skills. Please try to apply these principles this week. If you do, we guarantee they will improve the quality of your interactions.
   B. The enclosed handout on listening skills will be important improving the quality of your interactions. We guarantee it. All you have to do is take some time this week to read it and to consciously try to apply the principles. Listening skills are very important for managers, but they are not usually emphasized. Whenever managers are depicted in books, manuals or the media, they are always talking, never listening.

C. Listening well is one of the most important skills a manager can have, yet it's not usually given much attention. Think about any representation of managers in books, manuals, or in the media that you may have seen. They're always talking, never listening. We'd like you to read the enclosed handout on listening skills and consciously try to apply them the rest of the week. We guarantee you will see a difference in the quality of your interactions.

D. Effective listening, one very important tool in the effective manager's arsenal, is usually not emphasized enough. The usual depiction of managers in books, manuals or the media is one in which they are always talking, never listening. We'd like you to read the enclosed handout and consciously try to apply the information contained therein throughout the rest of the week. We feel sure that you will see a marked difference in the quality of your interactions.

2.   I. Chekhov wrote three dramatic masterpieces which share   2. __
certain themes and formats: Uncle Vanya, The Cherry Orchard, and The Three Sisters.

  II. They are primarily concerned with the passage of time and how this erodes human aspirations.

 III. The plays are haunted by the ghosts of the wasted life.

  IV. The characters are concerned with life's lesser problems; however, such as the inability to make decisions, loyalty to the wrong cause, and the inability to be clear.

   V. This results in a sweet, almost aching, type of a sadness referred to as Chekhovian.

A. Chekhov wrote three dramatic masterpieces: Uncle Vanya, The Cherry Orchard, and The Three Sisters. These masterpieces share certain themes and formats: the passage of time, how time erodes human aspirations, and the ghosts of wasted life. Each masterpiece is characterized by a sweet, almost aching, type of sadness that has become known as Chekhovian. The sweetness of this sadness hinges on the fact that it is not the great tragedies of life which are destroying these characters, but their minor flaws: indecisiveness, misplaced loyalty, unclarity.

B. The Cherry Orchard, Uncle Vanya, and The Three Sisters are three dramatic masterpieces written by Chekhov that use similar formats to explore a common theme. Each is primarily concerned with the way that passing time wears down human aspirations, and each is haunted by the ghosts of the wasted life. The characters are shown struggling futilely with the lesser problems of life: indecisiveness, loyalty to the wrong cause, and the inability to be clear. These struggles create a mood of sweet, almost aching, sadness that has become known as Chekhovian.

C. Chekhov's dramatic masterpieces are, along with The Cherry Orchard, Uncle Vanya, and The Three Sisters. These plays share certain thematic and formal similarities. They are concerned most of all with the passage of time and the way in which time erodes human aspirations. Each play is haunted by the specter of the wasted life. Chekhov's characters are caught, however, by life's lesser snares: indecisiveness, loyalty to the wrong cause, and unclarity. The characteristic mood is a sweet, almost aching type of sadness that has come to be known as Chekhovian.

D. A Chekhovian mood is characterized by sweet, almost aching, sadness. The term comes from three dramatic tragedies by Chekhov which revolve around the sadness of a wasted life. The three masterpieces (Uncle Vanya, The Three Sisters, and The Cherry Orchard) share the same theme and format. The plays are concerned with how the passage of time erodes human aspirations. They are peopled with characters who are struggling with life's lesser problems. These are people who are indecisive, loyal to the wrong causes, or are unable to make themselves clear.

3.   I. Movie previews have often helped producers decide   3.___
       what parts of movies they should take out or leave in.
   II. The first 1933 preview of King Kong was very helpful
       to the producers because many people ran screaming
       from the theater and would not return when four men
       first attacked by Kong were eaten by giant spiders.
  III. The 1950 premiere of Sunset Boulevard resulted in the
       filming of an entirely new beginning, and a delay of
       six months in the film's release.
   IV. In the original opening scene, William Holden was in
       a morgue talking with thirty-six other "corpses" about
       the ways some of them had died.
    V. When he began to tell them of his life with Gloria
       Swanson, the audience found this hilarious, instead
       of taking the scene seriously.

   A. Movie previews have often helped producers decide what
      parts of movies they should leave in or take out. For
      example, the first preview of King Kong in 1933 was
      very helpful. In one scene, four men were first
      attacked by Kong and then eaten by giant spiders.
      Many members of the audience ran screaming from the
      theater and would not return. The premiere of the
      1950 film Sunset Boulevard was also very helpful. In
      the original opening scene, William Holden was in a
      morgue with thirty-six other "corpses," discussing
      the ways some of them had died. When he began to
      tell them of his life with Gloria Swanson, the
      audience found this hilarious. They were supposed to
      take the scene seriously. The result was a delay of
      six months in the release of the film while a new
      beginning was added.

B. Movie previews have often helped producers decide whether they should change various parts of a movie. After the 1933 preview of <u>King Kong</u>, a scene in which four men who had been attacked by Kong were eaten by giant spiders was taken out as many people ran screaming from the theater and would not return. The 1950 premiere of <u>Sunset Boulevard</u> also led to some changes. In the original opening scene, William Holden was in a morgue talking with thirty-six other "corpses" about the ways some of them had died. When he began to tell them of his life with Gloria Swanson, the audience found this hilarious, instead of taking the scene seriously.

C. What do <u>Sunset Boulevard</u> and <u>King Kong</u> have in common? Both show the value of using movie previews to test audience reaction. The first 1933 preview of <u>King Kong</u> showed that a scene showing four men being eaten by giant spiders after having been attacked by Kong was too frightening for many people. They ran screaming from the theater and couldn't be coaxed back. The 1950 premiere of <u>Sunset Boulevard</u> was also a scream, but not the kind the producers intended. The movie opens with William Holden lying in a morgue discussing the ways they had died with thirty-six other "corpses." When he began to tell them of his life with Gloria Swanson, the audience couldn't take him seriously. Their laughter caused a six-month delay while the beginning was rewritten.

D. Producers very often use movie previews to decide if changes are needed. The premiere of <u>Sunset Boulevard</u> in 1950 led to a new beginning and a six-month delay in film release. At the beginning, William Holden and thirty-six other "corpses" discuss the ways some of them died. Rather than taking this seriously, the audience thought it was hilarious when he began to tell them of his life with Gloria Swanson. The first 1933 preview of <u>King Kong</u> was very helpful for its producers because one scene so terrified the audience that many of them ran screaming from the theater and would not return. In this particular scene, four men who had first been attacked by Kong were being eaten by giant spiders.

4.   I. It is common for supervisors to view employees as "things" to be manipulated.   4.___

II. This approach does not motivate employees, nor does the carrot-and-stick approach because employees often recognize these behaviors and resent them.

III. Supervisors can change these behaviors by using self-inquiry and persistence.

IV. The best managers genuinely respect those they work with, are supportive and helpful, and are interested in working as a team with those they supervise.

V. They disagree with the Golden Rule that says "he or she who has the gold makes the rules."

A. Some managers act as if they think the Golden Rule means "he or she who has the gold makes the rules." They show disrespect to employees by seeing them as "things" to be manipulated. Obviously, this approach does not motivate employees any more than the carrot-and-stick approach motivates them. The employees are smart enough to spot these behaviors and resent them. On the other hand, the managers genuinely respect those they work with, are supportive and helpful, and are interested in working as a team. Self-inquiry and persistence can change even the former type of supervisor into the latter.

B. Many supervisors fall into the trap of viewing employees as "things" to be manipulated, or try to motivate them by using a carrot-and-stick approach. These methods do not motivate employees, who often recognize the behaviors and resent them. Supervisors can change these behaviors, however, by using self-inquiry and persistence. The best managers are supportive and helpful, and have genuine respect for those with whom they work. They are interested in working as a team with those they supervise. To them, the Golden Rule is not "he or she who has the gold makes the rules."

C. Some supervisors see employees as "things" to be used or manipulated using a carrot-and-stick technique. These methods don't work. Employees often see through them and resent them. A supervisor who wants to change may do so. The techniques of self-inquiry and persistence can be used to turn him or her into the type of supervisor who doesn't think the Golden Rule is "he or she who has the gold makes the rules." They may become like the best managers who treat those with whom they work with respect and give them help and support. These are the managers who know how to build a team.

D. Unfortunately, many supervisors act as if their employees are objects whose movements they can position at will. This mistaken belief has the same result as another popular motivational technique -- the carrot-and-stick approach. Both attitudes can lead to the same result -- resentment from those employees who recognize the behaviors for what they are. Supervisors who recognize these behaviors can change through the use of persistence and the use of self-inquiry. It's important to remember that the best managers respect their employees. They readily give necessary help and support and are interested in working as a team with those they supervise. To these managers, the Golden Rule is not "he or she who has the gold makes the rules."

5.   I. The first half of the nineteenth century produced a
       group of pessimistic poets -- Byron, De Musset,
       Heine, Pushkin, and Leopardi.
   II. It also produced a group of pessimistic composers --
       Schubert, Chopin, Schumann, and even the later
       Beethoven.
 III. Above all, in philosophy, there was the profoundly
       pessimistic philosopher, Schopenhauer.
  IV. The Revolution was dead, the Bourbons were restored,
       the feudal barons were reclaiming their land, and
       progress everywhere was being suppressed, as the
       great age was over.
   V. "I thank God," said Goethe, "that I am not young in
       so thoroughly finished a world."

   A. "I thank God," said Goethe, "that I am not young in
so thoroughly finished a world." The Revolution was
dead, the Bourbons were restored, the feudal barons
were reclaiming their land, and progress everywhere
was being suppressed. The first half of the nineteenth century produced a group of pessimistic poets:
Byron, De Musset, Heine, Pushkin, and Leopardi. It
also produced pessimistic composers: Schubert, Chopin,
Schumann. Although Beethoven came later, he fits into
this group, too. Finally and above all, it also
produced a profoundly pessimistic philosopher,
Schopenhauer. The great age was over.

   B. The first half of the nineteenth century produced a
group of pessimistic poets: Byron, De Musset, Heine,
Pushkin, and Leopardi. It produced a group of
pessimistic composers: Schubert, Chopin, Schumann,
and even the later Beethoven. Above all, it produced
a profoundly pessimistic philosopher, Schopenhauer.
For each of these men, the great age was over. The
Revolution was dead, and the Bourbons were restored.
The feudal barons were reclaiming their land, and
progress everywhere was being suppressed.

   C. The great age was over. The Revolution was dead --
the Bourbons were restored, and the feudal barons
were reclaiming their land. Progress everywhere was
being suppressed. Out of this climate came a pro-
found pessimism. Poets, like Byron, De Musset,
Heine, Pushkin, and Leopardi; composers, like Schubert,
Chopin, Schumann, and even the later Beethoven; and,
above all, a profoundly pessimistic philosopher,
Schopenauer. This pessimism which arose in the first
half of the nineteenth century is illustrated by these
words of Goethe, "I thank God that I am not young in
so thoroughly finished a world."

   D. The first half of the nineteenth century produced a
group of pessimistic poets, Byron, De Musset, Heine,
Pushkin, and Leopardi -- and a group of pessimistic
composers, Schubert, Chopin, Schumann, and the later
Beethoven. Above all, it produced a profoundly

pessimistic philosopher, Schopenhauer. The great age
was over. The Revolution was dead, the Bourbons were
restored, the feudal barons were reclaiming their
land, and progress everywhere was being suppressed.
"I thank God," said Goethe, "that I am not young in
so thoroughly finished a world."

6.   I. A new manager sometimes may feel insecure about his 6.___
or her competence in the new position.
  II. The new manager may then exhibit defensive or arrogant behavior towards those one supervises, or the
new manager may direct overly flattering behavior
toward one's new supervisor.

    A. Sometimes, a new manager may feel insecure about his
or her ability to perform well in this new position.
The insecurity may lead him or her to treat others
differently. He or she may display arrogant or
defensive behavior towards those he or she supervises,
or be overly flattering to his or her new supervisor.
    B. A new manager may sometimes feel insecure about his or
her ability to perform well in the new position. He
or she may then become arrogant, defensive, or overly
flattering towards those he or she works with.
    C. There are times when a new manager may be insecure
about how well he or she can perform in the new job.
The new manager may also behave defensive or act in
an arrogant way towards those he or she supervises, or
overly flatter his or her boss.
    D. Sometimes, a new manager may feel insecure about his
or her ability to perform well in the new position.
He or she may then display arrogant or defensive
behavior towards those they supervise, or become
overly flattering towards their supervisors.

7.   I. It is possible to eliminate unwanted behavior by 7.___
bringing it under stimulus control -- tying the
behavior to a cue, and then never, or rarely, giving
the cue.
  II. One trainer successfully used this method to keep an
energetic young porpoise from coming out of her tank
whenever she felt like it, which was potentially
dangerous.
 III. Her trainer taught her to do it for a reward, in
response to a hand signal, and then rarely gave the
signal.

    A. Unwanted behavior can be eliminated by tying the
behavior to a cue, and then never, or rarely, giving
the cue. This is called stimulus control. One trainer
was able to use this method to keep an energetic
young porpoise from coming out of her tank by teaching
her to come out for a reward in response to a hand
signal, and then rarely giving the signal.

B. Stimulus control can be used to eliminate unwanted behavior. In this method, behavior is tied to a cue, and then the cue is rarely, if ever, given. One trainer was able to successfully use stimulus control to keep an energetic young porpoise from coming out of her tank whenever she felt like it -- a potentially dangerous practice. She taught the porpoise to come out for a reward when she gave a hand signal, and then rarely gave the signal.

C. It is possible to eliminate behavior that is undesirable by bringing it under stimulus control by tying behavior to a signal, and then rarely giving the signal. One trainer successfully used this method to keep an energetic young porpoise from coming out of her tank, a potentially dangerous situation. Her trainer taught the porpoise to do it for a reward, in response to a hand signal, and then would rarely give the signal.

D. By using stimulus control, it is possible to eliminate unwanted behavior by tying the behavior to a cue, and then rarely or never give the cue. One trainer was able to use this method to successfully stop a young porpoise from coming out of her tank whenever she felt like it. To curb this potentially dangerous practice, the porpoise was taught by the trainer to come out of the tank for a reward, in response to a hand signal, and then rarely given the signal.

8.   I. There is a great deal of concern over the safety of   8.___
commercial trucks, caused by their greatly increased role in serious accidents since federal deregulation in 1981.

II. Recently, 60 percent of trucks in New York and Connecticut and 70 percent of trucks in Maryland randomly stopped by state troopers failed safety inspections.

III. Sixteen states in the United States require no training at all for truck drivers.

A. Since federal deregulation in 1981, there has been a great deal of concern over the safety of commercial trucks, and their greatly increased role in serious accidents. Recently, 60 percent of trucks in New York and Connecticut, and 70 percent of trucks in Maryland failed safety inspections. Sixteen states in the United States require no training at all for truck drivers.

B. There is a great deal of concern over the safety of commercial trucks since federal deregulation in 1981. Their role in serious accidents has greatly increased. Recently, 60 percent of trucks randomly stopped in Connecticut and New York, and 70 percent in Maryland failed safety inspections conducted by state troopers. Sixteen states in the United States provide no training at all for truck drivers.

    C. Commercial trucks have a greatly increased role in serious accidents since federal deregulation in 1981. This has led to a great deal of concern. Recently, 70 percent of trucks in Maryland and 60 percent of trucks in New York and Connecticut failed inspection of those that were randomly stopped by state troopers. Sixteen states in the United States require no training for all truck drivers.

    D. Since federal deregulation in 1981, the role that commercial trucks have played in serious accidents has greatly increased, and this has led to a great deal of concern. Recently, 60 percent of trucks in New York and Connecticut, and 70 percent of trucks in Maryland randomly stopped by state troopers failed safety inspections. Sixteen states in the U.S. don't require any training for truck drivers.

9.   I. No matter how much some people have, they still feel   9.___
      unsatisfied and want more, or want to keep what they have forever.

   II. One recent television documentary showed several people flying from New York to Paris for a one-day shopping spree to buy platinum earrings, because they were bored.

  III. In Brazil, some people are ordering coffins that cost a minimum of $45,000 and are equipping them with deluxe stereos, televisions and other graveyard necessities.

    A. Some people, despite having a great deal, still feel unsatisfied and want more, or think they can keep what they have forever. One recent documentary on television showed several people enroute from Paris to New York for a one day shopping spree to buy platinum earrings, because they were bored. Some people in Brazil are even ordering coffins equipped with such graveyard necessities as deluxe stereos and televisions. The price of the coffins start at $45,000.

    B. No matter how much some people have, they may feel unsatisfied. This leads them to want more, or to want to keep what they have forever. Recently, a television documentary depicting several people flying from New York to Paris for a one day shopping spree to buy platinum earrings. They were bored. Some people in Brazil are ordering coffins that cost at least $45,000 and come equipped with deluxe televisions, stereos and other necessary graveyard items.

    C. Some people will be dissatisfied no matter how much they have. They may want more, or they may want to keep what they have forever. One recent television documentary showed several people, motivated by boredom, jetting from New York to Paris for a one-day shopping spree to buy platinum earrings. In Brazil, some people are ordering coffins equipped with deluxe stereos, televisions and other graveyard necessities. The minimum price for these coffins - $45,000.

D. Some people are never satisfied. No matter how much they have they still want more, or think they can keep what they have forever. One television documentary recently showed several people flying from New York to Paris for the day to buy platinum earrings because they were bored. In Brazil, some people are ordering coffins that cost $45,000 and are equipped with deluxe stereos, televisions and other graveyard necessities.

10.   I. A television signal or video signal has three parts. 10.___

    II. Its parts are the black-and-white portion, the color portion, and the synchronizing (sync) pulses, which keep the picture stable.

  III. Each video source, whether it's a camera or a video-cassette recorder, contains its own generator of these synchronizing pulses to accompany the picture that it's sending in order to keep it steady and straight.

  IV. In order to produce a clean recording, a video-cassette recorder must "lock-up" to the sync pulses that are part of the video it is trying to record, and this effort may be very noticeable if the device does not have genlock.

A. There are three parts to a television or video signal: the black-and-white part, the color part, and the synchronizing (sync) pulses, which keep the picture stable. Whether it's a video-cassette recorder or a camera, each each video source contains its own pulse that synchronizes and generates the picture it's sending in order to keep it straight and steady. A video-cassette recorder must "lock up" to the sync pulses that are part of the video it's trying to record. If the device doesn't have genlock, this effort must be very noticeable.

B. A video signal or television is comprised of three parts: the black-and-white portion, the color por-tion, and the the sync (synchronizing) pulses, which keep the picture stable. Whether it's a camera or a video-cassette recorder, each video source contains its own generator of these synchronizing pulses. These accompany the picture that it's sending in order to keep it straight and steady. A video-cassette recorder must "lock up" to the sync pulses that are part of the video it is trying to record in order to produce a clean recording. This effort may be very noticeable if the device does not have genlock.

C. There are three parts to a television or video signal: the color portion, the black-and-white portion, and the sync (synchronizing pulses). These keep the picture stable. Each video source, whether it's a video-cassette recorder or a camera, generates these synchronizing pulses accompanying the picture it's

sending in order to keep it straight and steady. If
a clean recording is to be produced, a video-cassette
recorder must store the sync pulses that are part of
the video it is trying to record. This effort may
not be noticeable if the device does not have genlock.

D. A television signal or video signal has three parts:
the black-and-white portion, the color portion, and
the synchronizing (sync) pulses. It's the sync
pulses which keep the picture stable, which accompany
it and keep it steady and straight. Whether it's a
camera or a video-cassette recorder, each video
source contains its own generator of these synchronizing pulses. To produce a clean recording, a
video-cassette recorder must "lock-up" to the sync
pulses that are part of the video it is trying to
record. If the device does not have genlock, this
effort may be very noticeable.

———

KEY (CORRECT ANSWERS)

1. C		6. A	
2. B		7. B	
3. A		8. D	
4. B		9. C	
5. D		10. D	

———

PREPARING WRITTEN MATERIALS

EXAMINATION SECTION

DIRECTIONS: Each question consists of a sentence which may be classified appropriately under one of the following four categories:
   A. Incorrect because of faulty grammar or sentence structure;
   B. Incorrect because of faulty punctuation;
   C. Incorrect because of faulty capitalization;
   D. Correct.

Examine each sentence carefully. Then, in the space at the right, indicate the letter preceding the category which is the BEST of the four suggested above. Each incorrect sentence contains only one type of error. Consider a sentence correct if it contains no errors, although there may be other correct ways of expressing the same thought.

TEST 1

1. All the employees, in this office, are over twenty-one years old.　　　1.___

2. Neither the clerk nor the stenographer was able to explain what had happened.　　　2.___

3. Mr. Johnson did not know who he would assign to type the order.　　　3.___

4. Mr. Marshall called her to report for work on saturday.　　　4.___

5. He might of arrived on time if the train had not been delayed.　　　5.___

6. Some employees on the other hand, are required to fill out these forms every month.　　　6.___

7. The supervisor issued special instructions to his subordinates to prevent their making errors.　　　7.___

8. Our supervisor Mr. Williams, expects to be promoted in about two weeks.　　　8.___

9. We were informed that prof. Morgan would attend the conference.　　　9.___

10. The clerks were assigned to the old building; the stenographers, to the new building.　　　10.___

11. The supervisor asked Mr. Smith and I to complete the work as quickly as possible.　　　11.___

12. He said, that before an employee can be permitted to leave, the report must be finished.　　　12.___

13. An adding machine, in addition to the three typewriters,   13._
     are needed in the new office.

14. Having made many errors in her work, the supervisor asked   14._
     the typist to be more careful.

15. "If you are given an assignment," he said, "you should   15._
     begin work on it as quickly as possible."

16. All the clerks, including those who have been appointed   16._
     recently are required to work on the new assignment.

17. The office manager asked each employee to work one   17._
     saturday a month.

18. Neither Mr. Smith nor Mr. Jones was able to finish his   18._
     assignment on time.

19. The task of filing these cards is to be divided equally   19._
     between you and he.

20. He is an employee whom we consider to be efficient.   20._

21. I believe that the new employees are not as punctual as   21._
     us.

22. The employees, working in this office, are to be congratu-   22._
     lated for their work.

23. The delay in preparing the report was caused, in his   23._
     opinion, by the lack of proper supervision and coordination.

24. John Jones accidentally pushed the wrong button and then   24._
     all the lights went out.

25. The investigator ought to of had the witness sign the   25._
     statement.

KEY (CORRECT ANSWERS)

1. B		11. A	
2. D		12. B	
3. A		13. A	
4. C		14. A	
5. A		15. D	
6. B		16. B	
7. D		17. C	
8. B		18. D	
9. C		19. A	
10. D		20. D	

21. A
22. B
23. D
24. D
25. A

TEST 2

Questions 1-10.

DIRECTIONS: Each of the following sentences may be classified under one of the following four options:
   A. Faulty; contains an error in grammar only
   B. Faulty; contains an error in spelling only
   C. Faulty; contains an error in grammar and an error in spelling
   D. Correct; contains no error in grammar or in spelling

Examine each sentence carefully to determine under which of the above four options it is BEST classified. Then, in the space at the right, write the letter preceding the option which is the best of the four listed above.

1. A recognized principle of good management is that an assignment should be given to whomever is best qualified to carry it out.   1.___

2. He considered it a privilege to be allowed to review and summarize the technical reports issued annually by your agency.   2.___

3. Because the warehouse was in an inaccessable location, deliveries of electric fixtures from the warehouse were made only in large lots.   3.___

4. Having requisitioned the office supplies, Miss Brown returned to her desk and resumed the computation of petty cash disbursements.   4.___

5. One of the advantages of this chemical solution is that records treated with it are not inflamable.   5.___

6. The complaint of this employee, in addition to the complaints of the other employees, were submitted to the grievance committee.   6.___

7. A study of the duties and responsibilities of each of the various categories of employees was conducted by an unprejudiced classification analyst.   7.___

8. Ties of friendship with this subordinate compels him to withold the censure that the subordinate deserves.   8.___

9. Neither of the agencies are affected by the decision to institute a program for rehabilitating physically handi-caped men and women.   9.___

10. The chairman stated that the argument between you and he   10._
    was creating an intolerable situation.

Questions 11-25.

DIRECTIONS: Each of the following sentences may be classified under
              one of the following four options:
              A. Correct
              B. Sentence contains an error in spelling
              C. Sentence contains an error in grammar
              D. Sentence contains errors in both grammar and
                 spelling.

11. He reported that he had had a really good time during his   11._
    vacation although the farm was located in a very
    inaccessible portion of the country.

12. It looks to me like he has been fasinated by that beautiful 12._
    painting.

13. We have permitted these kind of pencils to accumulate on   13._
    our shelves, knowing we can sell them at a profit of five
    cents apiece any time we choose.

14. Believing that you will want an unexagerated estimate of   14._
    the amount of business we can expect, I have made every
    effort to secure accurate figures.

15. Each and every man, woman and child in that untrameled   15._
    wilderness carry guns for protection against the wild
    animals.

16. Although this process is different than the one to which   16._
    he is accustomed, a good chemist will have no trouble.

17. Insensible to the fuming and fretting going on about him,   17._
    the engineer continued to drive the mammoth dynamo to its
    utmost capacity.

18. Everyone had studied his lesson carefully and was conse-   18._
    quently well prepared when the instructor began to discuss
    the fourth dimention.

19. I learned Johnny six new arithmetic problems this after-   19._
    noon.

20. Athletics is urged by our most prominent citizens as the   20._
    pursuit which will enable the younger generation to achieve
    that ideal of education, a sound mind in a sound body.

21. He did not see whoever was at the door very clearly but   21._
    thinks it was the city tax appraisor.

22. He could not scarsely believe that his theories had been   22.___
    substantiated in this convincing fashion.

23. Although you have displayed great ingenuity in carrying   23.___
    out your assignments, the choice for the position still
    lies among Brown and Smith.

24. If they had have pleaded at the time that Smith was an   24.___
    accessory to the crime, it would have lessened the
    punishment.

25. It has proven indispensible in his compilation of the   25.___
    facts in the matter.

———

KEY (CORRECT ANSWERS)

1. A		11. A	
2. D		12. D	
3. B		13. C	
4. D		14. B	
5. B		15. D	
6. A		16. C	
7. D		17. A	
8. C		18. B	
9. C		19. C	
10. A		20. A	

21. B
22. D
23. C
24. D
25. B

———

TEST 3

Questions 1-5.

DIRECTIONS: Questions 1 through 5 consist of sentences which may or may not contain errors in grammar or spelling or both. Sentences which do not contain errors in grammar or spelling or both are to be considered correct, even though there may be other correct ways of expressing the same thought. Examine each sentence carefully. Then, in the space at the right, write the letter of the answer which is the BEST of those suggested below:
   A. If the sentence is correct;
   B. If the sentence contains an error in spelling;
   C. If the sentence contains an error in grammar;
   D. If the sentence contains errors in both grammar and spelling.

1. Brown is doing fine although the work is irrevelant to his training.   1.__

2. The conference of sales managers voted to set its adjournment at one o'clock in order to give those present an opportunity to get rid of all merchandise.   2.__

3. He decided that in view of what had taken place at the hotel that he ought to stay and thank the benificent stranger who had rescued him from an embarassing situation.   3.__

4. Since you object to me criticizing your letter, I have no alternative but to consider you a mercenary scoundrel.   4.__

5. I rushed home ahead of schedule so that you will leave me go to the picnic with Mary.   5.__

Questions 6-15.

DIRECTIONS: Some of the following sentences contain an error in spelling, word usage, or sentence structure, or punctuation. Some sentences are correct as they stand although there may be other correct ways of expressing the same thought. All incorrect sentences contain only one error. Mark your answer to each question in the space at the right as follows:
   A. If the sentence has an error in spelling;
   B. If the sentence has an error in punctuation or capitalization;
   C. If the sentence has an error in word usage or sentence structure;
   D. If the sentence is correct.

6. Because the chairman failed to keep the participants from wandering off into irrelevant discussions, it was impossible to reach a consensus before the meeting was adjourned.   6.__

7. Certain employers have an unwritten rule that any appli-   7.___
   cant, who is over 55 years of age, is automatically
   excluded from consideration for any position whatsoever.

8. If the proposal to build schools in some new apartment   8.___
   buildings were to be accepted by the builders, one of
   the advantages that could be expected to result would be
   better communication between teachers and parents of
   schoolchildren.

9. In this instance, the manufacturer's violation of the   9.___
   law against deseptive packaging was discernible only to
   an experienced inspector.

10. The tenants' anger stemmed from the president's going to   10.___
    Washington to testify without consulting them first.

11. Did the president of this eminent banking company say;   11.___
    "We intend to hire and train a number of these disadvan-
    taged youths?"

12. In addition, today's confidential secretary must be   12.___
    knowledgable in many different areas: for example, she
    must know modern techniques for making travel arrangements
    for the executive.

13. To avoid further disruption of work in the offices, the   13.___
    protesters were forbidden from entering the building
    unless they had special passes.

14. A valuable secondary result of our training conferences   14.___
    is the opportunities afforded for management to observe
    the reactions of the participants.

15. Of the two proposals submitted by the committee, the   15.___
    first one is the best.

Questions 16-25.

DIRECTIONS: Each of the following sentences may be classified MOST
              appropriately under one of the following three categories:
                  A. Faulty because of incorrect grammar
                  B. Faulty because of incorrect punctuation
                  C. Correct

              Examine each sentence. Then, print the capital letter
              preceding the BEST choice of the three suggested above.
              All incorrect sentences contain only one type of error.
              Consider a sentence correct if it contains none of the
              types of errors mentioned, even though there may be
              other ways of expressing the same thought.

16. He sent the notice to the clerk who you hired yesterday.   16.___

17. It must be admitted, however that you were not informed   17.___
    of this change.

18. Only the employees who have served in this grade for at least two years are eligible for promotion.   18._

19. The work was divided equally between she and Mary.   19._

20. He thought that you were not available at that time.   20._

21. When the messenger returns; please give him this package.   21._

22. The new secretary prepared, typed, addressed, and delivered, the notices.   22._

23. Walking into the room, his desk can be seen at the rear.   23._

24. Although John has worked here longer than she, he produces a smaller amount of work.   24._

25. She said she could of typed this report yesterday.   25._

KEY (CORRECT ANSWERS)

1. D		11. B	
2. A		12. A	
3. D		13. C	
4. C		14. D	
5. C		15. C	
6. A		16. A	
7. B		17. B	
8. D		18. C	
9. A		19. A	
10. D		20. C	

21. B
22. B
23. A
24. C
25. A

TEST 4

Questions 1-5.

DIRECTIONS: Each of the following sentences may be classified MOST appropriately under one of the following three categories:
   A. Faulty because of incorrect grammar
   B. Faulty because of incorrect punctuation
   C. Correct

Examine each sentence. Then, print the capital letter preceding the BEST choice of the three suggested above. All incorrect sentences contain only one type of error. Consider a sentence correct if it contains none of the types of errors mentioned, even though there may be other correct ways of expressing the same thought.

1. Neither one of these procedures are adequate for the efficient performance of this task.   1.___

2. The typewriter is the tool of the typist; the cash register, the tool of the cashier.   2.___

3. "The assignment must be completed as soon as possible" said the supervisor.   3.___

4. As you know, office handbooks are issued to all new employees.   4.___

5. Writing a speech is sometimes easier than to deliver it before an audience.   5.___

Questions 6-15.

DIRECTIONS: Each statement given in Questions 6 through 15 contains one of the faults of English usage listed below. For each, choose from the options listed the MAJOR fault contained.
   A. The statement is not a complete sentence.
   B. The statement contains a word or phrase that is redundant.
   C. The statement contains a long, less commonly used word when a shorter, more direct word would be acceptable.
   D. The statement contains a colloquial expression that normally is avoided in business writing.

6. The fact that this activity will afford an opportunity to meet your group.   6.___

7. Do you think that the two groups can join together for next month's meeting?   7.___

8. This is one of the most exciting new innovations to be   8._
    introduced into our college.

9. We expect to consummate the agenda before the meeting ends   9._
    tomorrow at noon.

10. While this seminar room is small in size, we think we can   10._
    use it.

11. Do you think you can make a modification in the date of   11._
    the Budget Committee meeting?

12. We are cognizant of the problem but we think we can   12._
    ameliorate the situation.

13. Shall I call you around three on the day I arrive in the   13._
    City?

14. Until such time that we know precisely that the students   14._
    will be present.

15. The consensus of opinion of all the members present is   15._
    reported in the minutes.

Questions 16-25.

DIRECTIONS: For each of Questions 16 through 25, select from the
             options given below the MOST applicable choice.
             A. The sentence is correct.
             B. The sentence contains a spelling error only.
             C. The sentence contains an English grammar error onl
             D. The sentence contains both a spelling error and an
                English grammar error.

16. Every person in the group is going to do his share.   16._

17. The man who we selected is new to this University.   17._

18. She is the older of the four secretaries on the two   18._
    staffs that are to be combined.

19. The decision has to be made between him and I.   19._

20. One of the volunteers are too young for this complecated   20._
    task, don't you think?

21. I think your idea is splindid and it will improve this   21._
    report considerably.

22. Do you think this is an exaggerated account of the behavior   22._
    you and me observed this morning?

23. Our supervisor has a clear idea of excelence.   23._

24. How many occurences were verified by the observers? 24.___

25. We must complete the typing of the draft of the question- 25.___
aire by noon tomorrow.

KEY (CORRECT ANSWERS)

1. A			11. C	
2. C			12. C	
3. B			13. D	
4. C			14. A	
5. A			15. B	
6. A			16. A	
7. B			17. C	
8. B			18. C	
9. C			19. C	
10. B			20. D	

21. B
22. D
23. B
24. B
25. B

PHILOSOPHY, PRINCIPLES, PRACTICES, AND TECHNICS
OF
SUPERVISION, ADMINISTRATION, MANAGEMENT, AND ORGANIZATION
CONTENTS

CONTENTS (cont'd)

PHILOSOPHY, PRINCIPLES, PRACTICES, AND TECHNICS
OF
SUPERVISION, ADMINISTRATION, MANAGEMENT, AND ORGANIZATION

I. MEANING OF SUPERVISION

The extension of the democratic philosophy has been accompanied by an extension in the scope of supervision. Modern leaders and supervisors no longer think of supervision in the narrow sense of being confined chiefly to visiting employees, supplying materials, or rating the staff. They regard supervision as being intimately related to all the concerned agencies of society, they speak of the supervisor's function in terms of "growth", rather than the "improvement," of employees

This modern concept of supervision may be defined as follows:

Supervision is leadership and the development of leadership within groups which are cooperatively engaged in inspection, research, training, guidance and evaluation.

II. THE OLD AND THE NEW SUPERVISION

TRADITIONAL	MODERN
1. Inspection	1. Study and analysis
2. Focused on the employee	2. Focused on aims, materials, methods, supervisors, employees, environment
3. Visitation	3. Demonstrations, intervisitation, workshops, directed reading, bulletins, etc.
4. Random and haphazard	4. Definitely organized and planned (scientific)
5. Imposed and authoritarian	5. Cooperative and democratic
6. One person usually	6. Many persons involved (creative)

III. THE EIGHT (8) BASIC PRINCIPLES OF THE NEW SUPERVISION

1. *PRINCIPLE OF RESPONSIBILITY*

Authority to act and responsibility for acting must be joined.
   a. If you give responsibility, give authority.
   b. Define employee duties clearly.
   c. Protect employees from criticism by others.
   d. Recognize the rights as well as obligations of employees.
   e. Achieve the aims of a democratic society insofar as it is possible within the area of your work.
   f. Establish a situation favorable to training and learning.
   g. Accept ultimate responsibility for everything done in your section, unit, office, division, department.
   h. Good administration and good supervision are inseparable.

2. *PRINCIPLE OF AUTHORITY*

The success of the supervisor is measured by the extent to which the power of authority is not used.
   a. Exercise simplicity and informality in supervision.
   b. Use the simplest machinery of supervision.
   c. If it is good for the organization as a whole, it is probably justified.
   d. Seldom be arbitrary or authoritative.
   e. Do not base your work on the power of position or of personality.
   f. Permit and encourage the free expression of opinions.

3. *PRINCIPLE OF SELF-GROWTH*

The success of the supervisor is measured by the extent to which, and the speed with which, he is no longer needed.
   a. Base criticism on principles, not on specifics.
   b. Point out higher activities to employees.

    c. Train for self-thinking by employees, to meet new situations.
    d. Stimulate initiative, self-reliance and individual responsibility.
    e. Concentrate on stimulating the growth of employees rather than on removing defects.
4. *PRINCIPLE OF INDIVIDUAL WORTH*
    Respect for the individual is a paramount consideration in supervision.
    a. Be human and sympathetic in dealing with employees.
    b. Don't nag about things to be done.
    c. Recognize the individual differences among employees and seek opportunities to permit best expression of each personality.
5. *PRINCIPLE OF CREATIVE LEADERSHIP*
    The best supervision is that which is not apparent to the employee.
    a. Stimulate, don't drive employees to creative action.
    b. Emphasize doing good things.
    c. Encourage employees to do what they do best.
    d. Do not be too greatly concerned with details of subject or method.
    e. Do not be concerned exclusively with immediate problems and activities.
    f. Reveal higher activities and make them both desired and maximally possible.
    g. Determine procedures in the light of each situation but see that these are derived from a sound basic philosophy.
    h. Aid, inspire and lead so as to liberate the creative spirit latent in all good employees.
6. *PRINCIPLE OF SUCCESS AND FAILURE*
    There are no unsuccessful employees, only unsuccessful supervisors who have failed to give proper leadership.
    a. Adapt suggestions to the capacities, attitudes, and prejudices of employees.
    b. Be gradual, be progressive, be persistent.
    c. Help the employee find the general principle; have the employee apply his own problem to the general principle.
    d. Give adequate appreciation for good work and honest effort.
    e. Anticipate employee difficulties and help to prevent them.
    f. Encourage employees to do the desirable things they will do anyway.
    g. Judge your supervision by the results it secures.
7. *PRINCIPLE OF SCIENCE*
    Successful supervision is scientific, objective, and experimental. It is based on facts, not on prejudices.
    a. Be cumulative in results.
    b. Never divorce your suggestions from the goals of training.
    c. Don't be impatient of results.
    d. Keep all matters on a professional, not a personal level.
    e. Do not be concerned exclusively with immediate problems and activities.
    f. Use objective means of determining achievement and rating where possible.
8. *PRINCIPLE OF COOPERATION*
    Supervision is a cooperative enterprise between supervisor and employee.
    a. Begin with conditions as they are.
    b. Ask opinions of all involved when formulating policies.

        c. Organization is as good as its weakest link.
        d. Let employees help to determine policies and department
           programs.
        e. Be approachable and accessible - physically and mentally.
        f. Develop pleasant social relationships.
IV. WHAT IS ADMINISTRATION?
     Administration is concerned with providing the environment, the
material facilities,and the operational procedures that will promote
the maximum growth and development of supervisors and employees. (Organization is an aspect,and a concomitant,of administration.)
     There is no sharp line of demarcation between supervision and ad-
ministration; these functions are intimately interrelated and,often,
overlapping. They are complementary activities.
     1. *PRACTICES COMMONLY CLASSED AS "SUPERVISORY"*
        a. Conducting employees conferences
        b. Visiting sections,units,offices,divisions,departments
        c. Arranging for demonstrations
        d. Examining plans
        e. Suggesting professional reading
        f. Interpreting bulletins
        g. Recommending in-service training courses
        h. Encouraging experimentation
        i. Appraising employee morale
        j. Providing for intervisitation
     2. *PRACTICES COMMONLY CLASSIFIED AS "ADMINISTRATIVE"*
        a. Management of the office
        b. Arrangement of schedules for extra duties
        c. Assignment of rooms or areas
        d. Distribution of supplies
        e. Keeping records and reports
        f. Care of audio-visual materials
        g. Keeping inventory records
        h. Checking record cards and books
        i. Programming special activities
        j. Checking on the attendance and punctuality of employees
     3. *PRACTICES COMMONLY CLASSIFIED AS BOTH "SUPERVISORY" AND
        "ADMINISTRATIVE"*
        a. Program construction
        b. Testing or evaluating outcomes
        c. Personnel accounting
        d. Ordering instructional materials
V. RESPONSIBILITIES OF THE SUPERVISOR
     A person employed in a supervisory capacity must constantly be
able to improve his own efficiency and ability. He represents the
employer to the employees and only continuous self-examination can
make him a capable supervisor.
     Leadership and training are the supervisor's responsibility. An
efficient working unit is one in which the employees work with the
supervisor. It is his job to bring out the best in his employees.
He must always be relaxed,courteous and calm in his association with
his employees. Their feelings are important, and a harsh attitude
does not develop the most efficient employees.

VI. COMPETENCIES OF THE SUPERVISOR
   1. Complete knowledge of the duties and responsibilities of his position.
   2. To be able to organize a job, plan ahead and carry through.
   3. To have self-confidence and initiative.
   4. To be able to handle the unexpected situation and make quick decisions.
   5. To be able to properly train subordinates in the positions they are best suited for.
   6. To be able to keep good human relations among his subordinates.
   7. To be able to keep good human relations between his subordinates and himself and to earn their respect and trust.

VII. THE PROFESSIONAL SUPERVISOR-EMPLOYEE RELATIONSHIP

There are two kinds of efficiency: one kind is only apparent and is produced in organizations through the exercise of mere discipline; this is but a simulation of the second, or true, efficiency which springs from spontaneous cooperation. If you are a manager, no matter how great or small your responsibility, it is your job, in the final analysis, to create and develop this involuntary cooperation among the people whom you supervise. For, no matter how powerful a combination of money, machines, and materials a company may have, this is a dead and sterile thing without a team of willing, thinking and articulate people to guide it.

The following 21 points are presented as indicative of the exemplary basic relationship that should exist between supervisor and employee:
   1. Each person wants to be liked and respected by his fellow employee and wants to be treated with consideration and respect by his superior.
   2. The most competent employee will make an error. However, in a unit where good relations exist between the supervisor and his employees, tenseness and fear do not exist. Thus, errors are not hidden or covered up and the efficiency of a unit is not impaired.
   3. Subordinates resent rules, regulations, or orders that are unreasonable or unexplained.
   4. Subordinates are quick to resent unfairness, harshness, injustices and favoritism.
   5. An employee will accept responsibility if he knows that he will be complimented for a job well done, and not too harshly chastized for failure; that his supervisor will check the cause of the failure, and, if it was the supervisor's fault, he will assume the blame therefor. If it was the employee's fault, his supervisor will explain the correct method or means of handling the responsibility.
   6. An employee wants to receive credit for a suggestion he has made, that is used. If a suggestion cannot be used, the employee is entitled to an explanation. The supervisor should not say "no" and close the subject.
   7. Fear and worry slow up a worker's ability. Poor working environment can impair his physical and mental health. A good supervisor avoids forceful methods, threats and arguments to get a job done.
   8. A forceful supervisor is able to train his employees individually and as a team, and is able to motivate them in the proper channels.

4

9. A mature supervisor is able to properly evaluate his subordinates and to keep them happy and satisfied.
10. A sensitive supervisor will never patronize his subordinates.
11. A worthy supervisor will respect his employees' confidences.
12. Definite and clear-cut responsibilities should be assigned to each executive.
13. Responsibility should always be coupled with corresponding authority.
14. No change should be made in the scope or responsibilities of a position without a definite understanding to that effect on the part of all persons concerned.
15. No executive or employee, occupying a single position in the organization, should be subject to definite orders from more than one source.
16. Orders should never be given to subordinates over the head of a responsible executive. Rather than do this, the officer in question should be supplanted.
17. Criticisms of subordinates should, whever possible, be made privately, and in no case should a subordinate be criticized in the presence of executives or employees of equal or lower rank.
18. No dispute or difference between executives or employees as to authority or responsibilities should be considered too trivial for prompt and careful adjudication.
19. Promotions, wage changes, and disciplinary action should always be approved by the executive immediately superior to the one directly responsible.
20. No executive or employee should ever be required, or expected, to be at the same time an assistant to, and critic of, another.
21. Any executive whose work is subject to regular inspection should, whever practicable, be given the assistance and facilities necessary to enable him to maintain an independent check of the quality of his work.

III. MINI-TEXT IN SUPERVISION, ADMINISTRATION, MANAGEMENT, AND ORGANIZATION
A. BRIEF HIGHLIGHTS
Listed concisely and sequentially are major headings and important data in the field for quick recall and review.
1. *LEVELS OF MANAGEMENT*
Any organization of some size has several levels of management. In terms of a ladder the levels are:

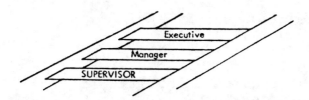

The first level is very important because it is the beginning point of management leadership.
2. *WHAT THE SUPERVISOR MUST LEARN*
A supervisor must learn to:
    (1) Deal with people and their differences
    (2) Get the job done through people
    (3) Recognize the problems when they exist
    (4) Overcome obstacles to good performance
    (5) Evaluate the performance of people
    (6) Check his own performance in terms of accomplishment

3. *A DEFINITION OF SUPERVISOR*
   The term supervisor means any individual having authority, in the interests of the employer, to hire,transfer,suspend,lay-off,recall, promote,discharge,assign,reward,or discipline other employees... or responsibility to direct them,or to adjust their grievances,or effectively to recommend such action,if, in connection with the foregoing, exercise of such authority is not of a merely routine or clerical nature but requires the use of independent judgment.

4. *ELEMENTS OF THE TEAM CONCEPT*
   What is involved in teamwork? The component parts are:
(1) Members	(3) Goals	(5) Cooperation
(2) A leader	(4) Plans	(6) Spirit

5. *PRINCIPLES OF ORGANIZATION*
   (1) A team member must know what his job is
   (2) Be sure that the nature and scope of a job are understood
   (3) Authority and responsibility should be carefully spelled out
   (4) A supervisor should be permitted to make the maximum number of decisions affecting his employees
   (5) Employees should report to only one supervisor
   (6) A supervisor should direct only as many employees as he can handle effectively
   (7) An organization plan should be flexible
   (8) Inspection and performance of work should be separate
   (9) Organizational problems should receive immediate attention
   (10) Assign work in line with ability and experience

6. *THE FOUR IMPORTANT PARTS OF EVERY JOB*
   (1) Inherent in every job is the *accountability* for results
   (2) A second set of factors in every job are *responsibilities*
   (3) Along with duties and responsibilities one must have the *authority* to act within certain limits without obtaining permission to proceed
   (4) No job exists in a vacuum. The supervisor is surrounded by key *relationships*

7. *PRINCIPLES OF DELEGATION*
   Where work is delegated for the first time,the supervisor should think in terms of these questions:
   (1) Who is best qualified to do this?
   (2) Can an employee improve his abilities by doing this?
   (3) How long should an employee spend on this?
   (4) Are there any special problems for which he will need guidance?
   (5) How broad a delegation can I make?

8. *PRINCIPLES OF EFFECTIVE COMMUNICATIONS*
   (1) Determine the media
   (2) To whom directed?
   (3) Identification and source authority
   (4) Is communication understood?

9. *PRINCIPLES OF WORK IMPROVEMENT*
   (1) Most people usually do only the work which is assigned to them
   (2) Workers are likely to fit assigned work into the time available to perform it
   (3) A good workload usually stimulates output
   (4) People usually do their best work when they know that results will be reviewed or inspected

  (5) Employees usually feel that someone else is responsible for conditions of work, workplace layout, job methods, type of tools and equipment, and other such factors
  (6) Employees are usually defensive about their job security
  (7) Employees have natural resistance to change
  (8) Employees can support or destroy a supervisor
  (9) A supervisor usually earns the respect of his people through his personal example of diligence and efficiency

10. *AREAS OF JOB IMPROVEMENT*

  The *areas* of job improvement are quite numerous, but the most common ones which a supervisor can identify and utilize are:

  (1) Departmental layout   (5) Work methods
  (2) Flow of work   (6) Materials handling
  (3) Workplace layout   (7) Utilization
  (4) Utilization of manpower (8) Motion economy

11. *SEVEN KEY POINTS IN MAKING IMPROVEMENTS*

  (1) Select the job to be improved
  (2) Study how it is being done now
  (3) Question the present method
  (4) Determine actions to be taken
  (5) Chart proposed method
  (6) Get approval and apply
  (7) Solicit worker participation

12. *CORRECTIVE TECHNIQUES OF JOB IMPROVEMENT*

Specific Problems	*General Problems*	*Corrective Technique*
(1) Size of workload	(1) Departmental layout	(1) Study with scale model
(2) Inability to meet schedules	(2) Flow of work	(2) Flow chart study
(3) Strain and fatigue	(3) Workplan layout	(3) Motion analysis
(4) Improper use of men and skills	(4) Utilization of manpower	(4) Comparison of units produced to standard allowances
(5) Waste, poor quality, unsafe conditions	(5) Work methods	(5) Methods analysis
(6) Bottleneck conditions that hinder output	(6) Materials handling	(6) Flow chart and equipment study
(7) Poor utilization of equipment and machines	(7) Utilization of equipment	(7) Down time vs. running time
(8) Efficiency and productivity of labor	(8) Motion economy	(8) Motion analysis

13. *A PLANNING CHECKLIST*

  (1) Objectives   (8) Equipment
  (2) Controls   (9) Supplies and materials
  (3) Delegations   (10) Utilization of time
  (4) Communications   (11) Safety
  (5) Resources   (12) Money
  (6) Methods and procedures (13) Work
  (7) Manpower   (14) Timing of improvements

14. *FIVE CHARACTERISTICS OF GOOD DIRECTIONS*

  In order to get results, directions must be:

  (1) Possible of accomplishment (4) Planned and complete
  (2) Agreeable with worker interests (5) Unmistakably clear
  (3) Related to mission

15. *TYPES OF DIRECTIONS*
    (1) Demands or direct orders   (3) Suggestion or implication
    (2) Requests   (4) Volunteering
16. *CONTROLS*
    A typical listing of the overall areas in which the supervisor should establish controls might be:
    (1) Manpower   (4) Quantity of work   (7) Money
    (2) Materials   (5) Time   (8) Methods
    (3) Quality of work   (6) Space
17. *ORIENTING THE NEW EMPLOYEE*
    (1) Prepare for him   (3) Orientation for the job
    (2) Welcome the new employee   (4) Follow-up
18. *CHECKLIST FOR ORIENTING NEW EMPLOYEES*

                                       Yes No

    (1) Do your appreciate the feelings of new employees when they first report for work? ... ...
    (2) Are you aware of the fact that the new employee must make a big adjustment to his job? ... ...
    (3) Have you given him good reasons for liking the job and the organization? ... ...
    (4) Have you prepared for his first day on the job? ... ...
    (5) Did you welcome him cordially and make him feel needed? ... ...
    (6) Did you establish rapport with him so that he feels free to talk and discuss matters with you? ... ...
    (7) Did you explain his job to him and his relationship to you? ... ...
    (8) Does he know that his work will be evaluated periodically on a basis that is fair and objective? .. ...
    (9) Did you introduce him to his fellow workers in such a way that they are likely to accept him? ... ...
    (10) Does he know what employee benefits he will receive? ... ...
    (11) Does he understand the importance of being on the job and what to do if he must leave his duty station? ... ...
    (12) Has he been impressed with the importance of accident prevention and safe practice? ... ...
    (13) Does he generally know his way around the department? ... ...
    (14) Is he under the guidance of a sponsor who will teach the right ways of doing things? ... ...
    (15) Do you plan to follow-up so that he will continue to adjust successfully to his job? ... ...
19. *PRINCIPLES OF LEARNING*
    (1) Motivation (2) Demonstration or explanation
    (3) Practice
20. *CAUSES OF POOR PERFORMANCE*
    (1) Improper training for job   (6) Lack of standards of performance
    (2) Wrong tools
    (3) Inadequate directions   (7) Wrong work habits
    (4) Lack of supervisory follow-up   (8) Low morale
    (5) Poor communications   (9) Other
21. *FOUR MAJOR STEPS IN ON-THE-JOB INSTRUCTION*
    (1) Prepare the worker   (3) Tryout performance
    (2) Present the operation   (4) Follow-up

22. *EMPLOYEES WANT FIVE THINGS*
   (1) Security   (2) Opportunity   (3) Recognition
   (4) Inclusion (5) Expression
23. *SOME DON'TS IN REGARD TO PRAISE*
   (1) Don't praise a person for something he hasn't done
   (2) Don't praise a person unless you can be sincere
   (3) Don't be sparing in praise just because your superior
       withholds it from you
   (4) Don't let too much time elapse between good performance
       and recognition of it
24. *HOW TO GAIN YOUR WORKERS' CONFIDENCE*
   Methods of developing confidence include such things as:
   (1) Knowing the interests, habits, hobbies of employees
   (2) Admitting your own inadequacies
   (3) Sharing and telling of confidence in others
   (4) Supporting people when they are in trouble
   (5) Delegating matters that can be well handled
   (6) Being frank and straightforward about problems and work-
       ing conditions
   (7) Encouraging others to bring their problems to you
   (8) Taking action on problems which impede worker progress
25. *SOURCES OF EMPLOYEE PROBLEMS*
   On-the-job causes might be such things as:
   (1) A feeling that favoritism is exercised in assignments
   (2) Assignment of overtime
   (3) An undue amount of supervision
   (4) Changing methods or systems
   (5) Stealing of ideas or trade secrets
   (6) Lack of interest in job
   (7) Threat of reduction in force
   (8) Ignorance or lack of communications
   (9) Poor equipment
   (10) Lack of knowing how supervisor feels toward employee
   (11) Shift assignments
   Off-the-job problems might have to do with:
   (1) Health   (2) Finances   (3) Housing   (4) Family
26. *THE SUPERVISOR'S KEY TO DISCIPLINE*
   There are several key points about discipline which the supervisor should keep in mind:
   (1) Job discipline is one of the disciplines of life and is
       directed by the supervisor.
   (2) It is more important to correct an employee fault than to
       fix blame for it.
   (3) Employee performance is affected by problems both on the
       job and off.
   (4) Sudden or abrupt changes in behavior can be indications of
       important employee problems.
   (5) Problems should be dealt with as soon as possible after
       they are identified.
   (6) The attitude of the supervisor may have more to do with
       solving problems than the techniques of problem solving.
   (7) Correction of employee behavior should be resorted to only
       after the supervisor is sure that training or counseling
       will not be helpful
   (8) Be sure to document your disciplinary actions.

(9) Make sure that you are disciplining on the basis of facts rather than personal feelings.

(10) Take each disciplinary step in order, being careful not to make snap judgments, or decisions based on impatience.

27. *FIVE IMPORTANT PROCESSES OF MANAGEMENT*

    (1) Planning   (2) Organizing   (3) Scheduling
    (4) Controlling   (5) Motivating

28. *WHEN THE SUPERVISOR FAILS TO PLAN*

    (1) Supervisor creates impression of not knowing his job
    (2) May lead to excessive overtime
    (3) Job runs itself-- supervisor lacks control
    (4) Deadlines and appointments missed
    (5) Parts of the work go undone
    (6) Work interrupted by emergencies
    (7) Sets a bad example
    (8) Uneven workload creates peaks and valleys
    (9) Too much time on minor details at expense of more important tasks

29. *FOURTEEN GENERAL PRINCIPLES OF MANAGEMENT*

(1) Division of work	(8) Centralization
(2) Authority and responsibility	(9) Scalar chain
(3) Discipline	(10) Order
(4) Unity of command	(11) Equity
(5) Unity of direction	(12) Stability of tenure of personnel
(6) Subordination of individual interest to general interest	(13) Initiative
(7) Remuneration of personnel	(14) Esprit de corps

30. *CHANGE*

Bringing about change is perhaps attempted more often, and yet less well understood, than anything else the supervisor does. How do people generally react to change? (People tend to resist change that is imposed upon them by other individuals or circumstances.)

Change is characteristic of every situation. It is a part of **every** real endeavor where the efforts of people are concerned.

  A. Why do people resist change?

    People may resist change because of:
      (1) Fear of the unknown
      (2) Implied criticism
      (3) Unpleasant experiences in the past
      (4) Fear of loss of status
      (5) Threat to the ego
      (6) Fear of loss of economic stability

  B. How can we best overcome the resistance to change?

    In initiating change, take these steps:
      (1) Get ready to sell
      (2) identify sources of help
      (3) Anticipate objections
      (4) Sell benefits
      (5) Listen in depth
      (6) Follow up

B. BRIEF TOPICAL SUMMARIES

I. WHO/WHAT IS THE SUPERVISOR?
   1. The supervisor is often called the "highest level employee and the lowest level manager."
   2. A supervisor is a member of both management and the work group. He acts as a bridge between the two.
   3. Most problems in supervision are in the area of human relations, or people problems.
   4. Employees expect: Respect, opportunity to learn and to advance, and a sense of belonging, and so forth.
   5. Supervisors are responsible for directing people and organizing work. Planning is of paramount importance.
   6. A position description is a set of duties and responsibilities inherent to a given position.
   7. It is important to keep the position description up-to-date and to provide each employee with his own copy.

II. THE SOCIOLOGY OF WORK
   1. People are alike in many ways; however each individual is unique.
   2. The supervisor is challenged in getting to know employee differences. Acquiring skills in evaluating individuals is an asset.
   3. Maintaining meaningful working relationships in the organization is of great importance.
   4. The supervisor has an obligation to help individuals to develop to their fullest potential.
   5. Job rotation on a planned basis helps to build versatility and to maintain interest and enthusiasm in work groups.
   6. Cross training (job rotation) provides backup skills.
   7. The supervisor can help reduce tension by maintaining a sense of humor, providing guidance to employees, and by making reasonable and timely decisions. Employees respond favorably to working under reasonably predictable circumstances.
   8. Change is characteristic of all managerial behavior. The supervisor must adjust to changes in procedures, new methods, technological changes, and to a number of new and sometimes challenging situations.
   9. To overcome the natural tendency for people to resist change, the supervisor should become more skillful in initiating change.

III. PRINCIPLES AND PRACTICES OF SUPERVISION
   1. Employees should be required to answer to only one superior.
   2. A supervisor can effectively direct only a limited number of employees, depending upon the complexity, variety, and proximity of the jobs involved.
   3. The organizational chart presents the organization in graphic form. It reflects lines of authority and responsibility as well as interrelationships of units within the organization.
   4. Distribution of work can be improved through an analysis using the "Work Distribution Chart."
   5. The "Work Distribution Chart" reflects the division of work within a unit in understandable form.
   6. When related tasks are given to an employee, he has a better chance of increasing his skills through training.
   7. The individual who is given the responsibility for tasks must also be given the appropriate authority to insure adequate results.
   8. The supervisor should delegate repetitive, routine work. Preparation of recurring reports, maintaining leave and attendance records are some examples.

9. Good discipline is essential to good task performance. Discipline is reflected in the actions of employees on the job in the absence of supervision.
10. Disciplinary action may have to be taken when the positive aspects of discipline have failed. Reprimand, warning, and suspension are examples of disciplinary action.
11. If a situation calls for a reprimand, be sure it is deserved and remember it is to be done in private.

IV. DYNAMIC LEADERSHIP
1. A style is a personal method or manner of exerting influence.
2. Authoritarian leaders often see themselves as the source of power and authority.
3. The democratic leader often perceives the group as the source of authority and power.
4. Supervisors tend to do better when using the pattern of leadership that is most natural for them.
5. Social scientists suggest that the effective supervisor use the leadership style that best fits the problem or circumstances involved.
6. All four styles -- telling, selling, consulting, joining -- have their place. Using one does not preclude using the other at another time.
7. The theory X point of view assumes that the average person dislikes work, will avoid it whenever possible, and must be coerced to achieve organizational objectives.
8. The theory Y point of view assumes that the average person considers work to be as natural as play, and, when the individual is committed, he requires little supervision or direction to accomplish desired objectives.
9. The leader's basic assumptions concerning human behavior and human nature affect his actions, decisions, and other managerial practices.
10. Dissatisfaction among employees is often present, but difficult to isolate. The supervisor should seek to weaken dissatisfaction by keeping promises, being sincere and considerate, keeping employees informed, and so forth.
11. Constructive suggestions should be encouraged during the natural progress of the work.

V. PROCESSES FOR SOLVING PROBLEMS
1. People find their daily tasks more meaningful and satisfying when they can improve them.
2. The causes of problems, or the key factors, are often hidden in the background. Ability to solve problems often involves the ability to isolate them from their backgrounds. There is some substance to the cliché that some persons "can't see the forest for the trees."
3. New procedures are often developed from old ones. Problems should be broken down into manageable parts. New ideas can be adapted from old ones.
4. People think differently in problem-solving situations. Using a logical, patterned approach is often useful. One approach found to be useful includes these steps:
   (a) Define the problem   (d) Weigh and decide
   (b) Establish objectives   (e) Take action
   (c) Get the facts   (f) Evaluate action

VI. TRAINING FOR RESULTS

1. Participants respond best when they feel training is important to them.
2. The supervisor has responsibility for the training and development of those who report to him.
3. When training is delegated to others, great care must be exercised to insure the trainer has knowledge, aptitude, and interest for his work as a trainer.
4. Training (learning) of some type goes on continually. The most successful supervisor makes certain the learning contributes in a productive manner to operational goals.
5. New employees are particularly susceptible to training. Older employees facing new job situations require specific training, as well as having need for development and growth opportunities.
6. Training needs require continuous monitoring.
7. The training officer of an agency is a professional with a responsibility to assist supervisors in solving training problems.
8. Many of the self-development steps important to the supervisor's own growth are equally important to the development of peers and subordinates. Knowledge of these is important when the supervisor consults with others on development and growth opportunities.

VII. HEALTH, SAFETY, AND ACCIDENT PREVENTION

1. Management-minded supervisors take appropriate measures to assist employees in maintaining health and in assuring safe practices in the work environment.
2. Effective safety training and practices help to avoid injury and accidents.
3. Safety should be a management goal. All infractions of safety which are observed should be corrected without exception.
4. Employees' safety attitude, training and instruction, provision of safe tools and equipment, supervision, and leadership are considered highly important factors which contribute to safety and which can be influenced directly by supervisors.
5. When accidents do occur they should be investigated promptly for very important reasons, including the fact that information which is gained can be used to prevent accidents in the future.

III. EQUAL EMPLOYMENT OPPORTUNITY

1. The supervisor should endeavor to treat all employees fairly, without regard to religion, race, sex, or national origin.
2. Groups tend to reflect the attitude of the leader. Prejudice can be detected even in very subtle form. Supervisors must strive to create a feeling of mutual respect and confidence in every employee.
3. Complete utilization of all human resources is a national goal. Equitable consideration should be accorded women in the work force, minority-group members, the physically and mentally handicapped, and the older employee. The important question is: "Who can do the job?"
4. Training opportunities, recognition for performance, overtime assignments, promotional opportunities, and all other personnel actions are to be handled on an equitable basis.

IX. IMPROVING COMMUNICATIONS

1. Communications is achieving understanding between the sender and the receiver of a message. It also means sharing information -- the creation of understanding.
2. Communication is basic to all human activity. Words are means of conveying meanings; however, real meanings are in people.
3. There are very practical differences in the effectiveness of one-way, impersonal, and two-way communications. Words spoken face-to-face are better understood. Telephone conversations are effective, but lack the rapport of person-to-person exchanges. The whole person communicates.
4. Cooperation and communication in an organization go hand-in-hand. When there is a mutual respect between people, spelling out rules and procedures for communicating is unnecessary.
5. There are several barriers to effective communications. These include failure to listen with respect and understanding, lack of skill in feedback, and misinterpreting the meanings of words used by the speaker. It is also common practice to listen to what we want to hear, and tune out things we do not want to hear.
6. Communication is management's chief problem. The supervisor should accept the challenge to communicate more effectively and to improve interagency and intra-agency communications.
7. The supervisor may often plan for and conduct meetings. The planning phase is critical and may determine the success or the failure of a meeting.
8. Speaking before groups usually requires extra effort. Stage fright may never disappear completely, but it can be controlled.

X. SELF-DEVELOPMENT

1. Every employee is responsible for his own self-development.
2. Toastmaster and toastmistress clubs offer opportunities to improve skills in oral communications.
3. Planning for one's own self-development is of vital importance. Supervisors know their own strengths and limitations better than anyone else.
4. Many opportunities are open to aid the supervisor in his developmental efforts, including job assignments; training opportunities, both governmental and non-governmental -- to include universities and professional conferences and seminars.
5. Programmed instruction offers a means of studying at one's own rate.
6. Where difficulties may arise from a supervisor's being away from his work for training, he may participate in televised home study or correspondence courses to meet his self-development needs.

XI. TEACHING AND TRAINING

A. The Teaching Process

Teaching is encouraging and guiding the learning activities of students toward established goals. In most cases this process consists in five steps: preparation, presentation, summarization, evaluation, and application.

1. Preparation

Preparation is twofold in nature; that of the supervi[sor] and the employee.

Preparation by the supervisor is absolutely essential t[o suc]cess. He must know what, when, where, how, and whom he will tea[ch]. Some of the factors that should be considered are:

(1) The objectives
(2) The materials needed
(3) The methods to be used
(4) Employee participation
(5) Employee interest
(6) Training aids
(7) Evaluation
(8) Summarization

Employee preparation consists in preparing the employee to receive the material. Probably the most important single factor in the preparation of the employee is arousing and maintaining his interest. He must know the objectives of the training, why he is there, how the material can be used, and its importance to him.

2. Presentation

In presentation, have a carefully designed plan and follow it. The plan should be accurate and complete, yet flexible enough to meet situations as they arise. The method of presentation will be determined by the particular situation and objectives.

3. Summary

A summary should be made at the end of every training unit and program. In addition, there may be internal summaries depending on the nature of the material being taught. The important thing is that the trainee must always be able to understand how each part of the new material relates to the whole.

4. Application

The supervisor must arrange work so the employee will be given a chance to apply new knowledge or skills while the material is still clear in his mind and interest is high. The trainee does not really know whether he has learned the material until he has been given a chance to apply it. If the material is not applied, it loses most of its value.

5. Evaluation

The purpose of all training is to promote learning. To determine whether the training has been a success or failure, the supervisor must evaluate this learning.

In the broadest sense evaluation includes all the devices, methods, skills, and techniques used by the supervisor to keep himself and the employees informed as to their progress toward the objectives they are pursuing. The extent to which the employee has mastered the knowledge, skills, and abilities, or changed his attitudes, as determined by the program objectives, is the extent to which instruction has succeeded or failed.

Evaluation should not be confined to the end of the lesson, day, or program but should be used continuously. We shall note later the way this relates to the rest of the teaching process.

B. Teaching Methods

A teaching method is a pattern of identifiable student and instructor activity used in presenting training material.

All supervisors are faced with the problem of deciding which method should be used at a given time.

ecture is direct oral presentation of material by the
isor. The present trend is to place less emphasis on the
er's activity and more on that of the trainee.
ssion
aching by discussion or conference involves using questions
other techniques to arouse interest and focus attention upon
tain areas, and by doing so creating a learning situation.
is can be one of the most valuable methods because it gives
e employees an opportunity to express their ideas and pool
heir knowledge.

Demonstration

The demonstration is used to teach how something works or how
to do something. It can be used to show a principle or what the
results of a series of actions will be. A well-staged demonstration is particularly effective because it shows proper methods
of performance in a realistic manner.

4. Performance

Performance is one of the most fundamental of all learning
techniques or teaching methods. The trainee may be able to tell
how a specific operation should be performed but he cannot be
sure he knows how to perform the operation until he has done so.

As with all methods, there are certain advantages and disadvantages
to each method.

5. Which Method to Use

Moreover, there are other methods and techniques of teaching.
It is difficult to use any method without other methods entering into it. In any learning situation a combination of methods
is usually more effective than any one method alone.

Finally, evaluation must be integrated into the other aspects of the
teaching-learning process.

It must be used in the motivation of the trainees; it must be used
to assist in developing understanding during the training; and it must
be related to employee application of the results of training.

This is distinctly the role of the supervisor.

———

ANSWER SHEET

EST NO. _____ PART _____ TITLE OF POSITION _____

(AS GIVEN IN EXAMINATION ANNOUNCEMENT - INCLUDE OPTION, IF ANY)

LACE OF EXAMINATION _____ DATE _____

(CITY OR TOWN)　　　　　　　　　　　　　　　　(STATE)

RATING

USE THE SPECIAL PENCIL.　MAKE GLOSSY BLACK MARKS.

	A B C D E		A B C D E		A B C D E		A B C D E		A B C D E
1	:: :: :: :: ::	26	:: :: :: :: ::	51	:: :: :: :: ::	76	:: :: :: :: ::	101	:: :: :: :: ::
2	:: :: :: :: ::	27	:: :: :: :: ::	52	:: :: :: :: ::	77	:: :: :: :: ::	102	:: :: :: :: ::
3	:: :: :: :: ::	28	:: :: :: :: ::	53	:: :: :: :: ::	78	:: :: :: :: ::	103	:: :: :: :: ::
4	:: :: :: :: ::	29	:: :: :: :: ::	54	:: :: :: :: ::	79	:: :: :: :: ::	104	:: :: :: :: ::
5	:: :: :: :: ::	30	:: :: :: :: ::	55	:: :: :: :: ::	80	:: :: :: :: ::	105	:: :: :: :: ::
6	:: :: :: :: ::	31	:: :: :: :: ::	56	:: :: :: :: ::	81	:: :: :: :: ::	106	:: :: :: :: ::
7	:: :: :: :: ::	32	:: :: :: :: ::	57	:: :: :: :: ::	82	:: :: :: :: ::	107	:: :: :: :: ::
8	:: :: :: :: ::	33	:: :: :: :: ::	58	:: :: :: :: ::	83	:: :: :: :: ::	108	:: :: :: :: ::
9	:: :: :: :: ::	34	:: :: :: :: ::	59	:: :: :: :: ::	84	:: :: :: :: ::	109	:: :: :: :: ::
10	:: :: :: :: ::	35	:: :: :: :: ::	60	:: :: :: :: ::	85	:: :: :: :: ::	110	:: :: :: :: ::

Make only ONE mark for each answer.　Additional and stray marks may be
counted as mistakes.　In making corrections, erase errors COMPLETELY.

	A B C D E		A B C D E		A B C D E		A B C D E		A B C D E
11	:: :: :: :: ::	36	:: :: :: :: ::	61	:: :: :: :: ::	86	:: :: :: :: ::	111	:: :: :: :: ::
12	:: :: :: :: ::	37	:: :: :: :: ::	62	:: :: :: :: ::	87	:: :: :: :: ::	112	:: :: :: :: ::
13	:: :: :: :: ::	38	:: :: :: :: ::	63	:: :: :: :: ::	88	:: :: :: :: ::	113	:: :: :: :: ::
14	:: :: :: :: ::	39	:: :: :: :: ::	64	:: :: :: :: ::	89	:: :: :: :: ::	114	:: :: :: :: ::
15	:: :: :: :: ::	40	:: :: :: :: ::	65	:: :: :: :: ::	90	:: :: :: :: ::	115	:: :: :: :: ::
16	:: :: :: :: ::	41	:: :: :: :: ::	66	:: :: :: :: ::	91	:: :: :: :: ::	116	:: :: :: :: ::
17	:: :: :: :: ::	42	:: :: :: :: ::	67	:: :: :: :: ::	92	:: :: :: :: ::	117	:: :: :: :: ::
18	:: :: :: :: ::	43	:: :: :: :: ::	68	:: :: :: :: ::	93	:: :: :: :: ::	118	:: :: :: :: ::
19	:: :: :: :: ::	44	:: :: :: :: ::	69	:: :: :: :: ::	94	:: :: :: :: ::	119	:: :: :: :: ::
20	:: :: :: :: ::	45	:: :: :: :: ::	70	:: :: :: :: ::	95	:: :: :: :: ::	120	:: :: :: :: ::
21	:: :: :: :: ::	46	:: :: :: :: ::	71	:: :: :: :: ::	96	:: :: :: :: ::	121	:: :: :: :: ::
22	:: :: :: :: ::	47	:: :: :: :: ::	72	:: :: :: :: ::	97	:: :: :: :: ::	122	:: :: :: :: ::
23	:: :: :: :: ::	48	:: :: :: :: ::	73	:: :: :: :: ::	98	:: :: :: :: ::	123	:: :: :: :: ::
24	:: :: :: :: ::	49	:: :: :: :: ::	74	:: :: :: :: ::	99	:: :: :: :: ::	124	:: :: :: :: ::
25	:: :: :: :: ::	50	:: :: :: :: ::	75	:: :: :: :: ::	100	:: :: :: :: ::	125	:: :: :: :: ::

ANSWER SHEET

TEST NO. _____ PART _____ TITLE OF POSITION _____

(AS GIVEN IN EXAMINATION ANNOUNCEMENT - INCLUDE OPTION, IF ANY)

PLACE OF EXAMINATION _____ DATE _____

(CITY OR TOWN)   (STATE)

RATING

USE THE SPECIAL PENCIL.   MAKE GLOSSY BLACK MARKS.

	A B C D E		A B C D E		A B C D E		A B C D E		A B C D E
1	⋮ ⋮ ⋮ ⋮ ⋮	26	⋮ ⋮ ⋮ ⋮ ⋮	51	⋮ ⋮ ⋮ ⋮ ⋮	76	⋮ ⋮ ⋮ ⋮ ⋮	101	⋮ ⋮ ⋮ ⋮ ⋮
2	⋮ ⋮ ⋮ ⋮ ⋮	27	⋮ ⋮ ⋮ ⋮ ⋮	52	⋮ ⋮ ⋮ ⋮ ⋮	77	⋮ ⋮ ⋮ ⋮ ⋮	102	⋮ ⋮ ⋮ ⋮ ⋮
3	⋮ ⋮ ⋮ ⋮ ⋮	28	⋮ ⋮ ⋮ ⋮ ⋮	53	⋮ ⋮ ⋮ ⋮ ⋮	78	⋮ ⋮ ⋮ ⋮ ⋮	103	⋮ ⋮ ⋮ ⋮ ⋮
4	⋮ ⋮ ⋮ ⋮ ⋮	29	⋮ ⋮ ⋮ ⋮ ⋮	54	⋮ ⋮ ⋮ ⋮ ⋮	79	⋮ ⋮ ⋮ ⋮ ⋮	104	⋮ ⋮ ⋮ ⋮ ⋮
5	⋮ ⋮ ⋮ ⋮ ⋮	30	⋮ ⋮ ⋮ ⋮ ⋮	55	⋮ ⋮ ⋮ ⋮ ⋮	80	⋮ ⋮ ⋮ ⋮ ⋮	105	⋮ ⋮ ⋮ ⋮ ⋮
6	⋮ ⋮ ⋮ ⋮ ⋮	31	⋮ ⋮ ⋮ ⋮ ⋮	56	⋮ ⋮ ⋮ ⋮ ⋮	81	⋮ ⋮ ⋮ ⋮ ⋮	106	⋮ ⋮ ⋮ ⋮ ⋮
7	⋮ ⋮ ⋮ ⋮ ⋮	32	⋮ ⋮ ⋮ ⋮ ⋮	57	⋮ ⋮ ⋮ ⋮ ⋮	82	⋮ ⋮ ⋮ ⋮ ⋮	107	⋮ ⋮ ⋮ ⋮ ⋮
8	⋮ ⋮ ⋮ ⋮ ⋮	33	⋮ ⋮ ⋮ ⋮ ⋮	58	⋮ ⋮ ⋮ ⋮ ⋮	83	⋮ ⋮ ⋮ ⋮ ⋮	108	⋮ ⋮ ⋮ ⋮ ⋮
9	⋮ ⋮ ⋮ ⋮ ⋮	34	⋮ ⋮ ⋮ ⋮ ⋮	59	⋮ ⋮ ⋮ ⋮ ⋮	84	⋮ ⋮ ⋮ ⋮ ⋮	109	⋮ ⋮ ⋮ ⋮ ⋮
10	⋮ ⋮ ⋮ ⋮ ⋮	35	⋮ ⋮ ⋮ ⋮ ⋮	60	⋮ ⋮ ⋮ ⋮ ⋮	85	⋮ ⋮ ⋮ ⋮ ⋮	110	⋮ ⋮ ⋮ ⋮ ⋮

Make only ONE mark for each answer.   Additional and stray marks may be counted as mistakes.   In making corrections, erase errors COMPLETELY.

	A B C D E		A B C D E		A B C D E		A B C D E		A B C D E
11	⋮ ⋮ ⋮ ⋮ ⋮	36	⋮ ⋮ ⋮ ⋮ ⋮	61	⋮ ⋮ ⋮ ⋮ ⋮	86	⋮ ⋮ ⋮ ⋮ ⋮	111	⋮ ⋮ ⋮ ⋮ ⋮
12	⋮ ⋮ ⋮ ⋮ ⋮	37	⋮ ⋮ ⋮ ⋮ ⋮	62	⋮ ⋮ ⋮ ⋮ ⋮	87	⋮ ⋮ ⋮ ⋮ ⋮	112	⋮ ⋮ ⋮ ⋮ ⋮
13	⋮ ⋮ ⋮ ⋮ ⋮	38	⋮ ⋮ ⋮ ⋮ ⋮	63	⋮ ⋮ ⋮ ⋮ ⋮	88	⋮ ⋮ ⋮ ⋮ ⋮	113	⋮ ⋮ ⋮ ⋮ ⋮
14	⋮ ⋮ ⋮ ⋮ ⋮	39	⋮ ⋮ ⋮ ⋮ ⋮	64	⋮ ⋮ ⋮ ⋮ ⋮	89	⋮ ⋮ ⋮ ⋮ ⋮	114	⋮ ⋮ ⋮ ⋮ ⋮
15	⋮ ⋮ ⋮ ⋮ ⋮	40	⋮ ⋮ ⋮ ⋮ ⋮	65	⋮ ⋮ ⋮ ⋮ ⋮	90	⋮ ⋮ ⋮ ⋮ ⋮	115	⋮ ⋮ ⋮ ⋮ ⋮
16	⋮ ⋮ ⋮ ⋮ ⋮	41	⋮ ⋮ ⋮ ⋮ ⋮	66	⋮ ⋮ ⋮ ⋮ ⋮	91	⋮ ⋮ ⋮ ⋮ ⋮	116	⋮ ⋮ ⋮ ⋮ ⋮
17	⋮ ⋮ ⋮ ⋮ ⋮	42	⋮ ⋮ ⋮ ⋮ ⋮	67	⋮ ⋮ ⋮ ⋮ ⋮	92	⋮ ⋮ ⋮ ⋮ ⋮	117	⋮ ⋮ ⋮ ⋮ ⋮
18	⋮ ⋮ ⋮ ⋮ ⋮	43	⋮ ⋮ ⋮ ⋮ ⋮	68	⋮ ⋮ ⋮ ⋮ ⋮	93	⋮ ⋮ ⋮ ⋮ ⋮	118	⋮ ⋮ ⋮ ⋮ ⋮
19	⋮ ⋮ ⋮ ⋮ ⋮	44	⋮ ⋮ ⋮ ⋮ ⋮	69	⋮ ⋮ ⋮ ⋮ ⋮	94	⋮ ⋮ ⋮ ⋮ ⋮	119	⋮ ⋮ ⋮ ⋮ ⋮
20	⋮ ⋮ ⋮ ⋮ ⋮	45	⋮ ⋮ ⋮ ⋮ ⋮	70	⋮ ⋮ ⋮ ⋮ ⋮	95	⋮ ⋮ ⋮ ⋮ ⋮	120	⋮ ⋮ ⋮ ⋮ ⋮
21	⋮ ⋮ ⋮ ⋮ ⋮	46	⋮ ⋮ ⋮ ⋮ ⋮	71	⋮ ⋮ ⋮ ⋮ ⋮	96	⋮ ⋮ ⋮ ⋮ ⋮	121	⋮ ⋮ ⋮ ⋮ ⋮
22	⋮ ⋮ ⋮ ⋮ ⋮	47	⋮ ⋮ ⋮ ⋮ ⋮	72	⋮ ⋮ ⋮ ⋮ ⋮	97	⋮ ⋮ ⋮ ⋮ ⋮	122	⋮ ⋮ ⋮ ⋮ ⋮
23	⋮ ⋮ ⋮ ⋮ ⋮	48	⋮ ⋮ ⋮ ⋮ ⋮	73	⋮ ⋮ ⋮ ⋮ ⋮	98	⋮ ⋮ ⋮ ⋮ ⋮	123	⋮ ⋮ ⋮ ⋮ ⋮
24	⋮ ⋮ ⋮ ⋮ ⋮	49	⋮ ⋮ ⋮ ⋮ ⋮	74	⋮ ⋮ ⋮ ⋮ ⋮	99	⋮ ⋮ ⋮ ⋮ ⋮	124	⋮ ⋮ ⋮ ⋮ ⋮
25	⋮ ⋮ ⋮ ⋮ ⋮	50	⋮ ⋮ ⋮ ⋮ ⋮	75	⋮ ⋮ ⋮ ⋮ ⋮	100	⋮ ⋮ ⋮ ⋮ ⋮	125	⋮ ⋮ ⋮ ⋮ ⋮